GAA Book of Days

Cusack & Hogan

Hawk Hill Publishing
Ireland

Hawk Hill Publishing

Cherryville, Kildare Town, Co. Kildare. Ireland

info@hawkhillpublishing.ie

First published by Hawk Hill Publishing 2008

Set in Bembo Book MT Pro

Typeset by Hawk Hill Publishing.

Printed in Italy by L.E.G.O. S.p.A.

ISBN 13: 978-0-9560163-0-0

January 1st

The Celtic Times Newspaper is launched on this day in 1887 with Michael Cusack as the editor. The newspaper was a weekly Gaelic games newspaper but it's run was short lived, closing up a little over a year later.

'Gaelic football is personal. It's not a kick around in the park early on a Sunday morning. It's not a run out for the boys.' Liam Hayes.

'Hurling is a terrific feeling. It doesn't matter about any other year. It is here. It is now. It is the moment. With half a minute to go, it is ours. That is savage. It is great crack. What else would you be doing? Ye think we are boring. But it is a hell of a thing and the supporters bring terrific elation. You cannot begin to touch that. It is just a terrific feeling and being involved with players who give it all, all of the time is serious.' Brian Cody, the Kilkenny Manager, on hurling.

January 2nd

Central council award Dublin the Leinster Senior football title, on this day in 1898, after a number of attempts to refix an earlier abandoned match fails.

Jack O'Shea of the St. Mary's club in Kerry won seven All-Ireland Senior medals with the Kingdom starting with his first in 1978 and his last in 1986. During this time he was named footballer of the year on no less than four occasions adding to six All Star accolades and it is no great surprise he was included on the 1984 Football Team of the Century but surprisingly was omitted from the Football Team of the Millennium in 1999.

'Their main discussion was on the Clare team which went on the lines that the Clare team were tinkers, Loughnane was a tramp and the Clare team must be on drugs.' Clare manager Ger Loughnane quotes an alleged overheard conversation among three priests at a match in 1998.

January 3rd

'He's had a chequered career really as regards his consistency in the blue shirt of Dublin but overall you'd have to say that Vinny Murphy has made his contribution to Dublin football and he should be proud of it.' Tom Carr on Vinnie Murphy who retired from Senior inter-county football on this day in 2002.

'To test the pulse of the nation, a hurling club was established in Dublin.' Michael Cusack in the United Ireland newspaper on this day in 1885.

'For example, we played five championship games in Croke Park and all that the Kildare players got after the Galway game was a ticket to go up to one of the executive suites where they got a drink and a few sandwiches and sausages. It is time for players to be invited for a meal in one of the boxes where they can relax and mingle after a game.' Mick O'Dwyer, then Kildare manager, on the reward for the 1998 All-Ireland finalists Kildare.

January 4th

The National Leagues in football and hurling were first introduced in 1925 being won by Laois in the football and Cork in the hurling.

Eddie Keher of the Rower Inistioge club in Kilkenny scored fourteen points in the 1963 All-Ireland Senior hurling final when they beat Waterford 4-17 to 6-8, ten came from frees. It was his first All-Ireland Senior medal and he would go on to win five more, he was the team captain in the 1969 final when they beat Cork 2-15 to 2-9. Remarkably he scored 2-11 in the 1971 final but was still on the losing side to Tipperary, 5-17 to 5-14. He was named at right full forward on the Team of the Millennium in 1999.

'I am sick, we may have played well, but we did not play well enough.' Nicky English the Tipperary hurler on losing to Galway in the All-Ireland semi-final in 1987 when they were beaten 3-20 to 2-17. Galway went on to beat Kilkenny in the final having lost the previous two finals.

January 5th

‘Well, I’m still getting great enjoyment out of it, and as long as I enjoy it I’ll keep with it. Simple as that.’ Mick O’Dwyer on this day in 2003, as manager of Laois he was enjoying fifty years of being involved in inter county football at different levels. Laois lost that day to Longford in the O’Byrne cup, 0-10 to 0-13.

‘Ordinary Catholics have nothing to fear from us. But the true enemies of Ulster will be targeted, and that’s a lot wider than just Sinn Fein and the IRA.’ Stated aim of the Orange Volunteers who on this day in 1999 injured a construction worker when they bombed a GAA club in Magherafelt.

‘They’ve total respect for the opposition, but they’re certainly not in awe of them.’ Tyrone manager Mickey Harte on his team’s confidence.

January 6th

'They tried to shaft me on three occasions.' Liam Austin the Cavan football manager explains why he resigned on this day in 1999.

Kildare won the much delayed 1905 Leinster Senior football final on this day in 1907 when they beat Louth 0-12 to 1-7. Kildare went on to beat Kerry in the final.

Seán O'Neill of Newry Mitchell's in Down scored a goal in the 1968 All-Ireland Senior football final against Kerry to help his team to a 2-12 to 1-13 victory. It was his third time to win an All-Ireland Senior medal being a key part of the 1960 team that brought the first ever Sam to the county and who did it again a year later. He was picked as the Footballer of the Year in 1968, was twice an All Star and was picked as part of the Football Team of the Century to mark the GAA centenary in 1984.

January 7th

'No one wants that. The players don't want that, the county board don't want that, management don't want that, so I suppose it is only to sort things out to make sure that it doesn't happen. It would make things very awkward if players were asked to come into the panel. Things would be awkward between fellas when they would be meeting each other after.' Cork hurler Ben O'Connor speaking on this day in 2008 on the suggestion that an underage or club team might be brought in to replace striking Cork hurlers, to avoid the county getting a suspension for missing fixtures while the players were on strike.

Of the 16 leaders executed after the 1616 rising six were GAA members.

'It's more enjoyable as a player but when you are two stone overweight and 44 years of age and going slow, winning one as a manager isn't bad either.' Páidí Ó Sé on winning the All-Ireland.

January 8th

‘But the coverage the game got was fantastic. Normal programmes, nothing to do with sport, were suddenly interested. That may not be all good, but it popularises the game. Controversy when it’s happening is terrible and people get cut up about it. But you look back and think: “Wasn’t it mighty?”’ Ger Loughnane on the controversy surrounding him in 1998.

‘You’d need to wear a gas mask at some under-age matches to avoid the smell of drink.’ Tommy Mullaney, GAA Board Secretary in Co Roscommon, on the problem of under-age drinking in the GAA.

‘In the future we would like to think that we’ll arrive at a situation where there’s harmony between the GPA and the GAA, and that a good close working relationship can be built.’ Dessie Farell Chief Executive of the GPA speaking in 2002.

January 9th

'That is the oldest section of the ground that is due for renewal, hopefully in the coming year.' GAA spokesperson on this day in 1997, confirming that a problem with mice in the canal end had been dealt with. The statement came after a hot dog concession was found guilty of thirty infringements of the food hygiene regulations on All-Ireland day the previous year.

Mick Lyons of Meath was the last football captain to lift the old Sam Maguire in 1987.

'The club titles were a family thing, but this is a sea of emotion.' Joe Kernan the Armagh manager compares winning three All-Ireland club finals, as the manager of Crossmaglen Rovers, to winning the All-Ireland Senior football final against Kerry in 2002.

January 10th

Official viewing figures released on this day in 2006 show that the most watched sporting event of the previous year was the All-Ireland Senior football final, between Tyrone and Kerry, with an estimated viewership of 887,000.

Mick Mackey of the Ahane club in Limerick was captain of the Senior hurlers in the 1936 final when they beat Kilkenny 5-6 to 1-5. Mackay had helped them on their way to the final when he scored five goals and three points against Tipperary in the Munster final that year. It was his second All-Ireland Senior medal and he would add another in 1940, adding to fifteen county hurling medals and five county football medals with his club. He was named as full forward on the Team of the Millennium in 1999.

'You know when your back is to the wall, when they get a few scores, and are on top of you, there is no place to hide.' Davy FitzGerald the Waterford hurling manager on playing Kilkenny in Croke Park.

January 11th

A strike by the Down Senior footballers and the team management ended on this day in 1998. The strike began the previous Friday when the players arrived to find the gates locked at Ballyholland and the pitch unplayable. Manager Peter McGrath informed the local press they were withdrawing their services. After talks with county officials and a change of training venue what was described as 'a simple misunderstanding' by the county board was resolved.

'Whenever a team loses, there's always a row at half-time but when they win, it's an inspirational speech.' John O'Mahony, Mayo and former Galway manager.

'Don't always be looking at the end result lads, enjoy the road a little. That was one of the greatest spins you could have there today. Good road, breathtaking scenery, the lot.' Ger Loughnane encourages his players to enjoy the journey.

January 12th

'You know, we have taken a lot of hidings from Tipp over the years but today we stuck with it and put them away.' Former Waterford manager Gerald McCarthy on beating Tipperary in the 1998 Munster semi-final.

'They will become the most successful team and in time will be seen as the greatest.' Waterford's Tony Mansfield on the 2008 All-Ireland Senior hurling champions Kilkenny.

In 1896 a goal in Gaelic games, which was previously worth five points, is reduced to three points.

'Armagh supporters probably expect us to be in an Ulster final. While it is good to be there, we want to try and do what hasn't been done before and get to an All-Ireland.' Joe Kernan before the Ulster final in 2002, Armagh would go on to win both Ulster and the All-Ireland that year

January 13th

‘There’s no doubt there’s enough of hurlers and fabulous structures for development. Dublin are going to win an All-Ireland soon, I mean within the next eight years.’ Michael O’Grady the Dublin hurling manager on this day in 1997.

Sligo won their first Connacht Senior football title since 1928 in 1975, unfortunately they ran into a very good Kerry team under the stewardship of Mick O’Dwyer for the first time in the championship. Sligo kept it respectable for most of the game but Kerry scored 3-2 in the last ten minutes of the game to give them a 3-13 to 0-5 win. In a way Sligo were possibly lucky, the championship had been reduced from the previous year’s eighty minutes to seventy for the 1975 campaign.

‘What we needed was to lose the fear of winning, not the fear of losing.’ Brian McEniff, Donegal manager on the 1992 All-Ireland Senior football final when they beat Dublin 0-18 to 0-14.

January 14th

'This is not an anti-media thing. It's just that the players felt that they had so many requests for interviews last year that it became a distraction.' Eamonn Cregan declares the Limerick hurlers a no-interview zone on this day in 2002.

The Celtic Times, the Gaelic games newspaper edited by Michael Cusack, ceases publication on this day in 1888.

Antrim become the first Ulster team to reach the All-Ireland Senior football final on this day in 1912, playing for the delayed 1911 championship. They were no match for Cork with Billy Mackessy scoring a hat trick of goals to help the Leesiders to a 6-6 to 1-2 scoreline.

'I never retired they just stopped picking me.' Tony Scullion, Derry full back on his retirement from the inter-county team.

January 15th

'The suggestion that people who play Gaelic sports or support them are more likely to be partial and prejudiced jurors than other groups of people is manifestly untenable.' Court documents submitted on this day in 1998 arguing that a case should not be moved because the defendant's company was the sponsor of the Armagh Senior football team and the prosecution's claim they would have difficulty finding an impartial jury in Newry was false.

Christy Ring was forty-three when he played his last Championship match for Cork in 1963. There was a clamour that he be recalled in 1966 when Cork reached the final but the player let it be known he felt he should not be picked. He continued to play club hurling for Glen Rovers until 1967.

'Arguably, the greatest weakness of the Association during the year was the lack of discipline at far too many games.' Liam Mulvihill former GAA Director-General speaking in 1998.

January 16th

'Of course, amateur status is an issue. It's always an issue. But from the point of view of the players' committee the feeling is that players aren't really looking to get paid. It's more of an expense issue rather than a pay-for-play issue.' GPA representative James Nallen on this day in 2002.

'There is no doubt about it, no point in denying it, that the powers-that-be in the GAA do not want Clare to win this All-Ireland.' Ger Loughnane prior to the 'replay' of the replay of the 1998 All-Ireland semi-final replay with Offaly brought about by the referee blowing the final whistle three minutes early.

'I saw thee start up and, snatching the hurley from the man nearest to thee, thou didst rush into the thick of the crowd and before sitting down thou didst win the goal three times on the men of Tara.' Translation from the ancient Irish story 'Tóraíocht Dhiarmada agus Ghráinne.'

January 17th

‘I gave up a lot of good friends and left a lot of good people. I was in Derry for a long time, but there was no opportunity to go and watch a match because we were reminded all the time about our personal security.’ Seán McNulty who won an All-Ireland Minor title with Down on how Rule 21 impacted on his life when he joined the RUC and had to give up his membership of the GAA.

The Original Rules 1885

‘Before commencing play hurlers shall draw up in two lines in the centre of the field opposite to each other and catch hands or hurleys across, then separate. The referee then throws the ball along the ground between the players or up high over their heads.’ The GAA agrees the new rules for the playing of Gaelic games at a meeting in Thurles on this day in 1885.

January 18th

Stradbally and Portarlington were suspended from the Laois Senior county league, where both were semi-finalists, and suspended from the following year's league by the County Board on this day in 1996. The suspension followed a league game between the two sides that erupted into a fight involving players and a club mentor from Portarlington as the second half started.

The first All-Ireland Under 21 Championship began in 1964. Kerry won the first ever football final beating Laois, 1-10 to 1-3, while Tipperary beat Wexford in the hurling final, 8-9 to 3-1.

'We may have come in the back door, but we're going out the front.' Offaly captain Hubert Rigney in 1998 after becoming the first team to lift the Liam McCarthy Cup having benefitted from the new 'back door' system introduced the previous year. Offaly Senior hurling titles: 1981, 1985, 1994, 1998.

January 19th

Wexford won their sixth Leinster Senior football title in a row on this day in 1919 when they beat Louth in the delayed 1918 final, 2-5 to 1-4. A record that still remains unbroken, matched by first Kildare then Dublin. Wexford then received a bye into the final, because of the flu pandemic sweeping the country at that time, where they won their famous four-in-a-row.

Antrim are know as The Saffrons or the Glensmen and have yet to win a Senior All-Ireland in either code but have contested All-Ireland semi-finals in both codes, the only Ulster team to do so.

'Action and discussions are taking place at the highest levels in the GAA and the general consensus is that we want the rule withdrawn nice and quietly.' Seán Kelly the then outgoing chairman of the Kerry County Board commenting on Rule 21, which bans members of the Crown forces or constabulary playing Gaelic games, on this day in 1998.

January 20th

‘I feel disappointed and disgusted at some of the shenanigans that went on. But it’s not the first time in the GAA and won’t be the last that this sort of thing has happened, but I don’t remember it before in Antrim.’ Gerry Barry, former Antrim county secretary, speaking on this day in 1997 on his removal at the previous weekend’s county convention.

Armagh are known as the Orchard County or Cathedral County and won their first All-Ireland in 2002

‘Had we won, I doubt if it would be accepted as graciously as under the old structure. There is a stigma attached to it which is greatly emphasised by many in the media, in particular when a prominent hurling county is the beneficiary.’ Tommy Barrett, Tipperary County Board Secretary, discusses the stigma attached to winning an All-Ireland by the ‘back door’ on this day in 1998. Tipperary lost the previous year’s All-Ireland Senior hurling final to Clare.

January 21st

Tipperary won the 1916 All-Ireland Senior hurling final played on this day in 1917, delayed due to the aftermath of the 1916 Rising. Playing that year in their famous blue and gold for the first time they had to come from behind to beat Kilkenny, 5-4 to 3-2. Kilkenny had not been beaten in a final since 1898 so it was suitable revenge for the Premier county who had lost their unbeaten record to the Cats in 1909.

Kildare withdrew from the GAA for a year in 1908 over an incident in the final of the Croke cup. After a Mayo goal the crowd invaded the pitch and Kildare refused to play on until the pitch was cleared. The referee awarded the game and trophy to Mayo, which led to Kildare's withdrawal from the association.

Under ancient Brehon Law offences committed within a recognised game of hurling were punishable under the code.

January 22nd

One of the earliest challenges to the GAA was from militant Sabbatarians trying to stop the breaking of the 1695 Sunday Observance Act under which playing games on a Sunday was prohibited. Spectators and teams were often attacked by mobs.

Carlow are known as the Dolmen County, Barrowsiders, Fighting Cocks or Scallion Eaters and have yet to win a Senior title but have one for Intermediate hurling. There are twenty-six clubs in the county.

'The Association's work has done more for Ireland than all the speeches of politicians for the past five years. Beside reviving our national sports, the GAA has also revived national memories, the names of its clubs perpetuating the memory of many great and good Irishmen.' Douglas Hyde 1892.

January 23rd

Stephen O'Neill winner of two All-Irelands and former footballer of the year with Tyrone retired from inter-county football on this day in 2008 aged 27. He would make a late comeback for the All-Ireland final against Kerry later in the same year to win a third All-Ireland.

Senior hurling and football championship matches are increased in duration from sixty to eighty minutes in 1970 until 1974 when, it is agreed for the 1975 championship, games will be seventy minutes.

'In post-mortems you always look at the details. If we had put on the socks on a different foot maybe we'd have been able to perform better. If we had stayed in the shower a little bit longer. Sure who's to know?' Pat O'Shea the Kerry manager speaking the week after they lost the All-Ireland final to Tyrone in 2008.

January 24th

'It is in the overall interest that there be a wide spread of teams among the winners and that new faces come to the forefront regularly. In this regard, the re-emergence of a team from Connacht and Ulster which would overcome the Munster and Leinster champions would be good for Gaelic football.' 1988 report to congress seems prophetic.

Larry Hussey Cribben who played for Kildare in the All-Ireland of 1919 was 41.

'When you're playing you just have to worry about yourself. Even though you're part of a team the most important thing for you is to get your game right. As a manager you're wondering, because there's so many different lads on the panel, what makes them tick; and then there's backroom staff and you've to make sure about the arrangements. It's very hard to keep on top of everything and to keep every player going.' Davy FitzGerald the Waterford hurling manager on management.

January 25th

'Use not henceforth the games which men call hurlings with clubs of a ball on the ground, from which great evils and maims have arisen, to the weakening of the defence of the said land.' The Statute of Kilkenny in 1366 banned colonists from playing the game of hurling as played by the Gaelic natives.

'At no time to use…the hurling of the little ball.' The Statute of Galway in 1537 suggests the earlier banning of hurling under the Statute of Kilkenny in 1366 had not worked.

'The players came to the conclusion that we had dug ourselves a hole, and now we had the choice over the final thirty-five minutes of whether we wanted to stay in it or climb out.' Cathal O'Rourke, the Armagh player, on being four points down at half time to Kerry in the 2002 All-Ireland Senior football final and the players view at that time. Armagh went on to win the final.

January 26th

Limerick won their second All-Ireland Senior hurling title on this day in 1918 when they beat Wexford, 9-5 to 1-3. It was Limerick's first time in a final since they had been disqualified in the 1911 final and their County Board suspended. Willie Gleeson scored three goals for Limerick in a game where you have to assume Wexford were distracted by the success of their footballers going for a record four-in-a-row that year.

Maurice Davin the first President of the GAA and one of the founding members died on this day in 1927 at the age of eighty-four.

'Unbelievable when that whistle went. In other years, we were on the wrong side of it. Thankfully, when the whistle went today, we weren't crying into the jersey. We were delighted.' Ken McGrath of Waterford speaking in 2008 on the county reaching the All-Ireland Senior hurling final for the first time since 1963.

January 27th

'There's a lot of pressure with that, but when you're going through it out there, my only thought was being thankful I was able to do that job, really, and that I wasn't going to be hiding in Kerry for the next couple of weeks if I hadn't done it.' Pat O' Shea the Kerry manager discusses the pressure of playing Cork in the 2007 All-Ireland Senior football final. Kerry Senior football titles: 1903, 1904, 1909, 1913, 1914, 1924, 1926, 1929, 1930,1931, 1932, 1937, 1939, 1940, 1941, 1946, 1953, 1955, 1959, 1962, 1969, 1970, 1975, 1978, 1979, 1980, 1981, 1984, 1985, 1986, 1997, 2000, 2004, 2006, 2007.

'I believed that Babs and I had an excellent working relationship. My mistake seems to have been to have accepted his resignation as a mature and well thought out decision rather than as a platform for a "Bring Back Babs campaign."' Seán Fogarty, outgoing Chairman of the Tipperary County Board, responds to criticism in Babs Keating's autobiography in 1997.

January 28th

'I still think he's the greatest midfielder ever.' Colm McAlarney the Down player giving his opinion of Mick O'Connell after he played against him in the 1968 All-Ireland Senior football final, Down won 2-12 to 2-13.

Wicklow County Council announce a £150,000 sponsorship deal with Wicklow GAA, for five years, on this day in 1999.

'We're like any town. There are sportsmen in every town, but they haven't achieved what we have. We've been labelled bandit country and still are to an extent. But what we have in Cross is some great sportsmen and great people.' Joe Kernan, Crossmaglen Rovers manager, speaking in 2000.

'Joe Brolly always talked a great game the problem is he didn't always play a great one.' Colm O'Rourke.

January 29th

A building strike holds up the building of the Cusack Stand and the 1937 All-Ireland Hurling final is moved to Fitzgerald Stadium where Tipperary beat Kilkenny 3-11 to 0-3.

'"If you want to even that up Sambo, I'll turn a blind eye" - a referee who knew I'd been hit, didn't see it, but wanted the game played fair. Tempting?' Antrim and All Star hurler Terence 'Sambo' McNaughton on refereeing.

'The game as it is played at present is fraught with danger and, so far as I can gather from looking on, it is simply, a helter-skelter, hit-or-miss business carried on without any attention to rules at all.' The 'Irish Sportsman' newspaper on the state of Gaelic games in 1891.

January 30th

Kilkenny were disqualified from the first ever All-Ireland Minor hurling championship in 1928 for failing to submit all the names and ages of their players to the Leinster Council. They had already beaten Wexford and Laois. Dublin became the first to win the Leinster Minor title but would lose out in the final, after a replay, to Cork.

Cavan are known as the Breffni County and won their first All-Ireland Senior football title in 1928 adding another four since.

'Brilliant game. A lot was said about the rivalry but it turned out exactly as I thought it would. Not a dirty stroke.' Ger Loughnane on the expected rivalry between Clare and Tipperary in the 1997 All-Ireland Senior hurling final. Clare won 0-20 to 2-13.

January 31st

'By the time we had eaten and headed to our hotel in a fairly sober state, the supporters had drunk the place dry and there was no draught left.' Richie Connor captain of the Offaly team, that deprived Kerry of a fifth-in-a-row All-Ireland title, on the challenge of getting a pint after the final in 1982.

The Ladies' Gaelic Football Association was founded in Hayes Hotel in Thurles in 1974 with Tipperary winning the first Ladies' All-Ireland, beating Offaly 2-3 to 2-2.

Nicky Rackard of the Wexford hurlers scored 7-7 against Antrim in the 1954 All-Ireland semi-final setting a record. Wexford were beaten by Cork in the final but won the next two All-Irelands in a row.

February 1st

'If I did I was thanking the man himself.' George O'Connor of Wexford explains why he dropped to his knees and blessed himself when the final whistle blew in the 1996 All-Ireland hurling final. With the defeat of Limerick it was his 17th championship season and made him the oldest man at thirty-six to win a first All-Ireland Senior hurling medal.

Derry play at Celtic Park with a capacity of 22,000.

'If I live to be a hundred I don't ever want to endure that kind of trauma again. Of all the hurling venues I've played in, none has ever unnerved me like the High Court managed to do that morning.' Nicky English of Tipperary compares hurling to the Irish legal system.

'Keep your eye on the ball, even when it's in the referee's pocket.' Christy Ring.

February 2nd

The First two teams to contest an inter-county game at what was to become Croke Park were Dublin and Kildare in February 1896, for the 1895 Leinster semi-final. The score was 2-7 to 0-4 to Dublin. Both counties were represented by club teams, Isles of the Sea and Clane, as was the custom of the time. Around 2000 spectators attended.

'The Association shall actively support the Irish language, traditional Irish dancing, music, song and other aspects of Irish culture.' Article 4 of the GAA.

'Before I go any further, I must point out that the game is not a punch up with a ball as an occasional distraction. Gaelic football is about skill and courage. The prime discipline is keeping your eye on the ball, despite the murderous attention of the opposition.' Simon Barnes of 'The London Times' newspaper explains Gaelic football to his readers.

February 3rd

Dublin play Tyrone in the first game under floodlights at Croke Park on this day in 2007.

The photograph of Michael Collins, Eamon de Valera and Arthur Griffith at the 1919 All-Ireland Senior hurling final when Cork beat Dublin in front of a crowd of 14,500 is the only one of the three of them together.

'Kids don't ask the coach whether he's an amateur or professional, they're just responding to you. You are their catalyst from the word go. Your enthusiasm brings on their enthusiasm.' Donal O'Grady the former Cork hurling manager.

'I'll have to look at it in the cold light. I don't like looking at games that we have lost in.' Limerick hurling manager Eamonn Cregan.

February 4th

‘Everyone has their day and I believe that I’ve had mine.’ DJ Carey announcing his retirement on this day in 1998 at the age of 27 having won two Senior All-Irelands, the retirement was to be thankfully short lived.

‘At the end of the day, Dublin isn’t going to pay Jason Sherlock to play and if he’s keen to pursue a full-time career in sport, that’s his own business.’ Tom Carr the former Dublin manager expresses his hope that Sherlock will continue to play for Dublin but points out some realities of the time, as the player heads to the New England Revolution soccer club for a two week training camp on this day in 1998.

‘If I had ducks they’d drown.’ Nicky English comments on a controversial draw in a Cork and Tipperary Munster final in Páirc Uí Chaoímh in 1991.

February 5th

Dublin for the first time in the history of the All-Ireland Senior football championship are not represented in the final by Young Ireland's on this day in 1899. The club had won three finals out of their four apprearances for the county up to then. Kickams instead had the honours and won the final of the 1897 championship against Cork, represented by Dunmanway, 2-6 to 0-2. William Guiry scord both goals for Dublin playing in a team mainly of drapers assistants.

'When I see a back page of a sports section with 'Semplegate Eight' and eight little pictures of the players involved, like criminals… these are players that have to go to work, that have to face family and they don't deserve that. I think that was an utter, utter disgrace and I would lay the blame at the CCC Committee for dealing with it in that method.' Cork hurling manager Gerald McCarthy on the coverage of suspensions handed down after a pre-match tussle with Clare in 2007.

February 6th

Limerick pick up their second, and last to date, All-Ireland Senior football title on this day in 1898. Playing for the delayed 1896 championship Limerick's Bill Murphy scored the only goal of the game to give his side a 1-5 to 0-7 victory. A year earlier the same goal would have been worth five points but it was still enough for a one point win one year later.

Sam Maguire, after whom the All-Ireland football trophy is named, dies on this day in 1927. An active member and past Chairman of the London GAA Board he was also the Chief Intelligence Officer for the IRB in Britain.

'We are getting closer but, listen, second is no place.' Conor Counihan the Cork football manager on another defeat to Kerry.

February 7th

The GAA publishes its rules for playing Gaelic football in the United Ireland on this day in 1885. The original time for championship games would remain sixty minutes until 1970.

'I know what it's like to get out of jail now and I've never been in it. I just told the Ballina boys I was too embarrassed to go into their dressing room because we didn't deserve to win that match.' Joe Kernan the Crossmaglen manager on winning the All-Ireland club football final in 1999 when they beat Ballina Stephenites 0-9 to 0-8.

<u>The Original Rules 1885</u>

Pushing or tripping from behind, holding from behind or butting with the head, shall be deemed foul, and the player so offending will be ordered to stand aside, and may not afterwards take part in the match, nor can his side substitute another man.

February 8th

'If Cork get to the final this year they should play it in Lourdes after what happened last weekend.' Colm O'Rourke on the Cork footballers late comeback in the 2008 semi-final against Kerry. Cork lost the replay 2-13 to 3-14 saving the GAA a trip to Lourdes.

'I wouldn't have decided to come to Laois unless I felt there was a huge amount of football potential in the county and obviously this result shows that I made the correct decision.' Mick O'Dwyer on Laois beating Kildare in the Leinster final, 2-13 to 1-13, in 2003.

The Original Rules 1885

The captains of each side shall toss for choice of sides before commencing play, and the players shall stand in two ranks opposite each other until the ball is thrown up, each man holding the hand of one of the other side

February 9th

'I knew they wouldn't be back the following evening if Tipp won, they were going on the beer.' Delegate, Paul McKenna, puts forward his club's side of the issue. Tipperary club Borrisokane were fined £50 for not turning up for their Junior B hurling final on the Monday following Tipperary's defeat of Wexford in the All-Ireland hurling semi-final.

The Monaghan football team is arrested by B specials on their way to the Ulster final, to play Derry, in 1922 and spend six weeks in prison.

The Original Rules 1885

The time of the actual play will be one hour. Sides to be changed only at half time.

February 10th

Dublin appeared in their fourth All-Ireland Senior football final in a row and won their third title in a row on this day in 1901, the first football team to do so. They were playing for the much delayed 1899 championship and beat Cork 1-10 to 0-6. Dublin were represented by the Geraldines while Cork were represented by the Nils club. Dublin Senior football titles: 1891, 1892, 1894, 1897, 1898, 1899, 1901, 1902, 1906, 1907, 1908, 1921, 1922, 1923, 1942, 1958, 1963, 1974, 1976, 1977, 1983, 1995.

The qualifier round is introduced in Senior Championship football for the first time in 2000 guaranteeing all teams at least two games.

<u>The Original Rules 1885</u>

There shall not be less than fifteen or more than twenty-one players aside.

February 11th

Ireland play France in rugby at Croke Park on this day in 2007. The first such game ever played at Croke Park after the ending of Rule 42, which banned competing non-Gaelic games from being played at GAA grounds. Ireland lost 20-17.

Footballer Brian Carbery becomes Carlow's first winner of the Eircell Vodafone GAA player of the month award on this day in 2002. The accolade came after Carlow's success in beating Wicklow in the final of the O'Byrne Cup, in the previous month.

'I am just hoping that they, the GAC, realise that they made a disastrous blunder. When you make a disastrous blunder you look at it again and you remedy that blunder.' Ger Loughnane attacking the GAA for its rule governing pitch encroachment during the All-Ireland hurling final.

February 12th

'Look, we won three Munster titles with Justin coming from playing Division Two hurling back in 1997. You don't forget that. We had great times with Justin. We have respect for him. And I hope, and I am sure, he is happy for us. Davy came in the first day with unbelievable passion and enthusiasm. He played like that as well. It is a pure professional set-up and the attention to detail is top notch. He is a double All-Ireland medal winner and we knew he had it in him.' Ken McGrath of Waterford on reaching the All-Ireland after a controversial year of changed managers in 2008.

'We don't want this dispute going on because it's going to tear the county apart and we don't want that. We want our players out on the field as soon as possible.' Bob Ryan, Cork County Board Press Officer, announces the Cork County Board voted to enter into binding arbitration to end the players' strike in the county, on this day in 2008.

February 13th

‘Everyone is looking at women’s Gaelic football as a serious thing now, it’s no joke anymore and it’s not a reason just to get the women out of the kitchen - they’re playing it because they want to win.’ Waterford footballer Noreen Walsh.

Sean Ryan President of the GAA from 1928 to 1932 was only thirty years of age when he took up the position becoming the youngest man to do so. In 1931 Congress asked him to stay on for an extra year rather than serving the normal three years.

Extra time was made compulsory for replays for the first time in 1926.

‘I received your letter this morning and I burned it.’ Michael Cusack in reply to a letter from the IAAA to propose amalgamation of the two athletic organizations.

February 14th

'It is with a feeling of sincere regret I now believe the present football management team should step aside and thereby contribute their assistance in resolving this dispute.' Chief Executive of the Labour Relations Commission Kieran Mulvey on the deal he brokered to end the strike by Cork players on this day in 2008.

The first All-Ireland Minor championship in hurling was played in 1928 with the football starting in 1929. Clare were the first winners in football beating Longford, 5-3 to 3-5, while Cork were the hurling champions beating Dublin in a replay 7-6 to 4-0.

'There's a few myths about me going around that I'm not this and I'm not that, but when I get committed then I put an awful lot of effort into it.' Vinnie Murphy of Dublin maybe suggests there were times when he was not committed.

February 15th

‘He was a giant and inspiration both on and off the field of play.’ Joe McDonagh the president of the GAA on Kerry great Johnny Walsh from Ballylongford, who passed away in 1998 at the age of eighty-eight. At the time of his death he was the president of the Kerry County Board. He won five Senior All-Ireland medals with Kerry, in 1932, 1937, 1939, 1940 and 1941. In the 1947 All-Ireland final played on this day in the Polo Grounds in New York, where Kerry and Cavan met, he was the manager of the Kerry team. Cavan won the match 2-11 to 2-7.

Mattie Power won six Senior All-Irelands with Kilkenny between 1922 and 1935 but also won one with Dublin in 1927.

‘Croke Park have never consulted me about anything, they would be afraid because they consider me a bit of a radical.’ Mick O’Dwyer in a radio interview in 2000.

February 16th

Wexford appeared in their sixth All-Ireland Senior football final in a row on this day in 1919. They beat Tipperary 0-5 to 0-6 to win the 1918 championship and their fourth title in a row. They were represented by the Blues and Whites club while Tipperary were represented by Fethard. Wexford have yet to appear in another All-Ireland Senior football final. Tipperary which was under martial law at the time of the match, coming shortly after the start of the War of Independence in that county, had to train in Waterford and only had the services of republican Tommy Ryan because he had been released from prison in time.

Michael Cusack refereed a game between North Tipperary and South Galway in the Phoenix Park on this day in 1886. Tipperary won with the only score of the game a single goal.

The first All-Ireland Championships begin in 1887 with five counties lining out in the hurling and eight in the football.

February 17th

‘The hardest things you must do in training will serve you well in the game, because you will never have to do them as hard again.’ Christy Ring.

Brendan Bracken whose father was a founding member of the GAA in 1884, J.K. Bracken of Templemore, would become an MP, member of the British war cabinet, a First Lord of the Admiralty and Viscount Bracken of Christchurch.

‘I told him they had honoured a man I considered to be an absolute traitor to this county for his part in the Jimmy Cooney incident in 1998 when he betrayed the interests of County Clare on that day.’ Ger Loughnane, the former Clare manager, on this day in 2006, on the reason for his exclusion by the County Board from an awards ceremony.

February 18th

On this day in 1912 Limerick and Kilkenny turned up in Cork with twelve thousand supporters to play the final of the delayed 1911 All-Ireland Senior hurling final. Unfortunately the officials ruled the pitch unplayable and postponed the game. Limerick disputing the call took to the field and claimed the game which led to a contorversey that would only end with the suspension of the Limerick County Board, the title being awarded to Kilkenny and eventually an alternative final being arranged between Kilkenny and the beaten Munster finalists Tipperary which the Cats won.

William Spain won an All-Ireland Senior hurling title with Limerick in 1887 and a Senior football title with Laois in 1889.

'For all the good we are doing for the language we might as well be a Chinese Athletic Association.' Joseph Skeffington at a Tyrone GAA convention in 1955.

February 19th

'Look it. This is the Mecca of the game. It's like reaching the promised land.' Seán Boylan on what it means to win the All-Ireland.

'You have to try and impart that on players in Waterford who like to play a good game or maybe do okay. But for me, maybe it was too severe. Maybe I have a one-track mind, only trying to win all the time. I didn't want to come second. I wanted to be first. I tried to push that on players constantly. It doesn't always wear well. Some of the older players mightn't like it.' Justin McCarthy on his departure from the Waterford team in June 2008.

Thomas St. George McCarthy one of the founding members of the GAA in 1884 later became a District Inspector of Constabulary, a position that by the turn of the century would have seen him banned from involvement in GAA games under Rule 21.

February 20th

Cork are known as the Rebel county and have won thirty All-Irelands in hurling and six in football. In 1890 and 1990 they won both.

'After the game the fans they were very disappointed, but very supportive. When you get that far you think you'll be back next year to finish off the job. But Sligo beat us in the first round in 1981 and we haven't been back in the All-Ireland since.' Danny Murray the Roscommon footballer. He was a member of the side which won four Connacht titles in a row between 1977 and 1980 and captained the side which made the breakthrough to the All-Ireland final in 1980.

'Beating Dublin in Croke Park is the benchmark of excellence.' Mick O'Dwyer.

February 21st

Aidan McAnespie, while crossing the border to attend a match in Aughnacloy between his club Aghaloo and Killeshil, was shot dead by British forces on this day in 1988.

'They go down by about €100 each decade. Programmes from the 1940s and 1950s are hard to come by but even early 1960s finals are collectable, they can fetch €20 to €50 for both football and hurling.' Mr. Peter Geoffroy, speaking on this day in 2002, on the value of All-Ireland match programmes. A 1920s GAA programme went for €570 in a previous sale.

'The satisfaction for me comes from the medals. That's what it's all about. I just want to win as many medals as I can while I'm playing.' Paul Galvin Kerry footballer.

February 22nd

Ballaghadereen of Mayo founded in 1885, is one of the oldest clubs in the county and had to wait forty-four years for their first title, winning the Junior championship in 1929. Between 1968 and 1972 they won Minor, Under-21, Junior and Intermediate titles. In 1972, their first year in the Senior grade, they were crowned county champions.

When Mayo and Meath met in the All-Ireland Senior football final in 1951 interest was so great that an official attendance of 78,201 was returned bringing in £9,334 and 11 shillings. The meeting between the same two sides in 1996 and the subsequent replay brought in an estimated £4 million.

Flags are first introduced into Gaelic games in 1895 so the linesmen could attract the attention of the referee.

February 23rd

Gaelic teams were first reduced to fifteen-a-side in 1913 and resulted in a football game between Kerry and Louth many claim was one of the greatest, calls were made for a further reduction to thirteen.

Annascaul GAA club in Kerry was formed in the mid 1950s when two parishes joined together. In 1957 they won the West Kerry championship with a team that included Seamus and Sean Murphy, who won six All-Irelands with Kerry between 1955 and 1970. In 1993, their first year in the Senior grade, they were defeated in the county final by Laune Rangers.

'It's a no-win situation for Down. Even if we beat Antrim no one will be impressed.' John Murphy a Down football selector explaining how you're damned if you don't and not very impressive if you do.

February 24th

Ireland play England in rugby at Croke Park on this day in 2007 where 'God Save the Queen' was played for the first time to respectful silence. Ireland won 43 - 13.

Tackling a player not in possession of the ball is banned in 1975.

Larry Stanley won an All-Ireland with Kildare in 1919 another with Dublin in 1923 and went on to represent Ireland at the 1924 Paris Olympics in athletics. In 1981 he was given an All Time Award at the All-Stars Banquet.

'If we produce another bad performance like that the show is over and my time with Galway is over. It will be exit stage left because it will show that my message is not getting through. If something is not working it's better to get somebody else.' Ger Loughnane sets the standard. Galway Senior hurling titles: 1923, 1980, 1987, and 1988.

February 25th

‘When the cows are casting their hair, they pull it off their backs and with their hands work it into large balls that grow very hard. This ball they use at the hurling which they strike with a stick called the commaan about three foot and a half in the handle. At the lower end it is crooked and about three inches broad, and on this part you may sometimes see one of the gamesters carry the ball tossing it for 40 or 50 yards in spite of all the adverse players: and when he is like to lose it, he generally gives it a great stroke to drive it towards the goal. Sometimes if he misses his blow at the ball, he knocks one of the opposers down, at which no resentment is to be shown.’ John Dunton describes hurling in Kildare in 1698.

The first International Rules test series was introduced in 1984 with Australia winning the first series 2-1.

The sideline puck was first introduced in 1899.

February 26th

‘Who has not heard that hurling is a dangerous game? It is the most dangerous game ever played on the planet. The game was invented by the most sublimely energetic and warlike race that the world has ever known.’ Michael Cusack, in the Celtic Times newspaper on this day in 1887.

‘He was a fine tennis and five player, a most extraordinary fine hurler and very fond of all those things.’ Description of Dudley Crosby, an Elizabethan planter from Laois, on his death in 1729.

‘Players have more of a semi-pro attitude. People ask me about pastimes but, in fairness, you don’t have any time for pastimes.’ Pa Laide of Kerry on the commitment required in the modern game of Gaelic football.

February 27th

The very first draw for the All-Ireland Senior Championship in hurling and football takes place on this day in 1887. Only counties who had formed county committees were eligible to play. The football draw was made up of: Wicklow, Clare, Wexford, Galway, Dublin, Tipperary, Cork, Kilkenny, Waterford, Louth, Limerick and Meath. Only five counties fielded teams in the first hurling competition: Clare, Wexford, Galway, Tipperary and Kilkenny.

Tipperary win their second National League hurling title, on this day in 1949, after a gap of twenty-two years. Pat Stakelum the Tipperary captain knocked in two goals past the Cork goalkeeper Tom Mulachy to set the Premier county up for a double tally, they won the All-Ireland later in the same year. The final score was 3-5 to 3-3.

William Guiry won an All-Ireland with Limerick in 1896 and another with Dublin in 1897.

February 28th

Dublin won their first All-Ireland Senior football title on this day in 1892 against Cork. Cork were represented by Clondrohid, the county champions, as was the custom at the time. The match played at Clonturk Park was for the delayed 1891 championship. Cork left the field thinking they were the winners with a score line of 2-9 to Dublin's 2-1 but after the game the referee stated he had disallowed a Cork goal. As a goal was worth more than any number of points at that time Dublin were the winners, 2-1 to 1-9. Given the controversial decision it was agreed there would be a replay but Clondrohid had ceased to exist before the replay could be arranged, and the result was left to stand.

A year after their first All-Ireland win Dublin went on to win their second title in 1892. They were represented in both years by the Young Irelands club from the Guinness brewery.

The Leinster football final in 1928 when Kildare beat Dublin saw a gate of 15,000 and receipts of £857.

March 1st

Kerry pick up their third National League football title on this day in 1931 when they beat Cavan, 1-3 to 1-2. John Joe Landers scored the goal for Kerry in the second half to secure the win.

In the famous 'Thunder and Lightning' final of 1939 when Kilkenny beat Cork 2-7 to 3-3 Jimmy Phelan scored 2-1 for Kilkenny and was on the team beaten by Limerick in the 1940 final.

'It was a big problem. You're trying to play matches and people are walking around the field with guns and helicopters are coming in. Thank God, that is all in the past and now everyone can look forward to the games.' Joe Kernan, on times past with Crossmaglen Rovers.

March 2nd

Ballygar represent Roscommon in Hurling but Galway in football

Both Kilkenny and Tipperary had to bow out from the 1941 All-Ireland hurling championship because of that year's foot-and-mouth epidemic. Cork won the first of four titles in a row that year when they beat Dublin.

'Given the television commentary of last Sunday's Minor hurling championship game between Galway and Tipperary in English rather than Irish was a decision taken by RTÉ without agreement with the Association.' GAA statement after the 2001 Minor hurling semi-final was broadcast in English.

'Everyone will have to do a little bit extra and if that happens, we can win.' Sean Cullinane the Waterford Senior hurler on what it takes to win a Munster final.

March 3rd

'That was very serious for us. We wouldn't have been left back into the county if we'd lost that game.' Paul Galvin of Kerry on playing Cork in the All-Ireland Senior football final in 2007.

Oliver Gough won an All-Ireland with Wexford in 1955 and another with Kilkenny in 1963.

Kerry won their solitary All-Ireland Senior hurling final in 1892 when they beat Wexford for the delayed 1891 championship. The game had ended in a controversial draw when the referee blew up as a Wexford free was literally sailing over the bar. It was agreed to play extra time with the Kingdom winning 2-3 to 1-5. Kerry were represented by Ballyduff and Wexford by Crossbeg.

March 4th

The Liam McCarthy Cup was presented for the first time on this day in 1923. It was presented to Limerick the All-Ireland Senior hurling champions who beat Dublin in the delayed 1921 championship decider, the score was 8-5 to 3-2, with Bob McConkey scoring four of the goals.

'What have Sinn Féin and Tyrone got in common? Sinn Féin have a better chance of seeing an All-Ireland.' Colm O'Rourke, speaking before the 2003 final when Tyrone won 0-12 to 0-9 against Armagh.

'There was no point in doing the interviews. It was a done deal anyway. How could they interview Justin, to be fair about it? I'd say it was he who interviewed them.' Richie Bennis on why he didn't seek an interiew for a third term prior to being replaced by Justine McCarthy as Limerick Senior hurling manager in October 2008.

March 5th

Garret Howard won three Senior All-Irelands with Limerick between 1921 and 1936 but also won two with Dublin in the same period.

Limerick won their first All-Ireland Senior hurling final in thirty-three years in 1973 beating Kilkenny, 1-21 to 1-14. Limerick had beaten surprise semi-finalists London, with the help of a Richie Bennis penalty, to reach the final. Limerick have yet to win another All-Ireland.

Croke Park's Nally Stand has been re-erected at Páirc Colmcille, home of Carrickmore in Tyrone.

'All-Ireland final day is fantastic, but only if you win it. We've been here in losing dressing rooms, and we certainly didn't want that feeling again.' Declan O'Sullivan Kerry team captain explains the motivation.

March 6th

'I just walked off the pitch. I honestly didn't realise everything that had gone on. I took some heavy punches to the head and I remember asking Kevin O'Neill questions about what went on. It took 10 minutes at least before I knew what had happened.' Liam McHale of Mayo discusses some confusion after his sending off in the 1996 All-Ireland final.

The first Railway cups were played in 1927.

'He wanted to come back. I felt he was entitled to come back. What the respective roles were will always remain a bit of a mystery. Some people think it was a good idea. Some people think it wasn't a good idea but the point was we were all fairly united at that stage. Unfortunately, it didn't end well in '78 because we got a hammering from Kerry in the final.' Tony Hanahoe former Dublin player-manager on Kevin Heffernan's return to the managers position the year after Hanahoe's team had won the 1977 All-Ireland.

March 7th

'No figure was ever mentioned, I don't know where that figure came from and it was all a bit presumptuous. I think it was exploiting the All-Ireland champions for some publicity.' Kerry chairman Sean Walsh on a press release by Gaelic Gear claiming to be in discussions about a €1 million deal with the All-Ireland football champions on this day in 2005.

The All-Ireland club championships were first started in 1971. East Kerry won the first football final and Roscrea won the hurling.

'We all know in Clare that he doesn't like us.' Clare hurling team manager Ger Loughnane taking umbrage with the All-Ireland hurling final analysis provided by Eamonn Cregan on RTE in 1997.

March 8th

‘I think any judges of football will say there’s not going to be a whole load of difference between Division One and Division Two football next year.’ Paul Caffrey the former Dublin manager takes a positive view of relegation in 2007.

Donegal play at Fr. Tierney Park, Ballyshannon along with Páirc Mac Cumhaill, Ballybofey with a capacity of 11,000 and 17,500 each.

‘I wouldn’t swap the last few months, over the last seven or eight years I’ve won Munster titles and a national league, awards here and there but the last three months have topped it for me. To get to an All-Ireland final. I mean, I’ll never forget running out on that field ‘til the day I die.’ John Mullane the Waterford hurler takes a positive view after losing to Kilkenny in the 2008 All-Ireland Senior final.

March 9th

Croke Park receives planning permission for redevelopment on this day in 1992.

John Connolly of Castlegar was captain of the Galway Senior hurlers when they won the National League in 1975, he won an All-Ireland with the team in 1980 and in the same year won the All-Ireland Senior Club hurling final with his local team. The 1980 All-Ireland was the first time the tribesmen had raised the McCarthy cup since 1927 and Connolly played alongside his two brothers Michael and team captain Joe.

'All ye scribes continue to write Kildare off. They are supposed to be whingers and toothless. But I think they proved out there today that they are great players.' Mick O'Dwyer.

March 10th

‘I was certain it was over even if a mistake had been made because I thought the referee’s decision was final. It wasn’t until nine or ten that night that I realised something was afoot and that there was going to be a replay.’ Ger Loughnane comments on the All-Ireland Senior hurling semi-final of 1998, which the referee Jimmy Cooney blew up three minutes early.

Derry are known as the Oak Leaf County, Foylesiders or the maiden city and won their first and only All-Ireland Senior football title in 1993 when they beat Cork in the final.

‘The voice of the players must be heard.’ Sean McCague incoming president of the GAA in April 2000.

March 11th

'It has been a long time coming and we have been a long time laying to rest certain ghosts. Now that we have this one won, we can get on with things.' Páidí Ó Sé, former Kerry manager, on Kerry's first All-Ireland title in 11 years.

'We take serious issue with any group which would negotiate a sponsorship deal on behalf of our members as long as they remain members of our organisation.' Joe McDonagh the GAA president on the GPA in March 2000.

'I make no bones about it they may be gone past their sell-by date. I appreciate that is probably going to cause a headline or two. But so be it.' Nicky Brennan spells out the possible end of the Railway Cups in 2008.

'Times have moved on. It's a pity the Board has not moved with the times.' Larry Tompkins of Cork.

March 12th

Michael Collins was Secretary of the London GAA club the Geraldine's from 1909 to 1915, he won four straight hurling championships with the Gers.

'Central Council's managerial ability is virtually negligible. We operated in an inefficient, inexpert and unprofessional way. Our organisational structures, systems and operations are out-of-date for the modern GAA.' Derry chairman Seamus McCloy expresses some concern with Croke Park management.

'I think the GAA have decided not to go down that road . . . they are not into the professional game and personally I wouldn't like to see that ever happen.' Bertie Ahern.

March 13th

Ballyconnell's First Ulsters playing their first game on this day in 1886 were warned by the local constabulary that they were breaking the Sunday Observance Act of 1605. While Sabbatarianism was a problem everywhere in the early days of the association Ulster teams suffered the brunt of the attention.

Thirty-two of Dr. Crokes's club members were in action in Easter Week 1916.

'I know I've changed over the years and I think it's for the better. I've probably toned down in the last year or so. Up to then I was very fiery.' Meath footballer Graham Geraghty referring to some fiery incidents in his playing time with the county.

March 14th

'In clubs in Dublin frequented by Catholics and Protestants, skittles and rackets are played on Sundays. The skittle-alley and the racket court are open to rich people, but the fields of Ireland are not to be opened to the people of Ireland the same day. This impudent absurdity will be removed by the GAA.' Michael Cusack in the United Ireland newspaper on this day in 1885 on the laws, which forbid Sunday games.

The new 'Hill 16' and 'Nally End' terrace are officially opened by GAA President, Seán Kelly, on this day in 2005. Bringing the official capacity of Croke Park to 82,300 spectators.

St. Vincent's club in Dublin which have provided such greats as Kevin Heffernan, Brian Mullins, Jimmy Keaveney, Tony Hanahoe and Ollie Freaney to the game won every Senior club title between 1949 and 1962 and an All-Ireland club title on this day in 1976 when they beat Roscommon Gaels 4-10 to 0-5.

March 15th

Tipperary won the first All-Ireland Senior football final to be played at Jones' Road, now the site of Croke Park, on this day in 1896. They were represented by Arravale Rovers who were playing for the delayed 1895 championship against Meath, represented by Pierce O'Mahony's. The score was 0-4 to 0-5. On the same day Tipperary, represented by Tubberadora, won the All-Ireland Senior hurling title for 1895; also the first hurling final at the future home of the GAA. Tipperary were the second team to win both codes in the one year, after Cork had done the same fives years earlier. Kilkenny making their second appearance in a hurling final were the opponents losing once again by a big margin, 6-8 to 1-0. Seven counties had played in the championship that year but Cork the reigning champions had stayed out in a dispute over football.

Cavan won seventeen out of nineteen Ulster Senior football finals between 1931 and 1949 when they lifted the Sam Maguire four times.

March 16th

'I don't agree with the theories that players can't keep going because of the physical demands. Material demands are more likely to cause a strain and end careers early. There's no reason why the body can't be kept in shape for ten years between, say, 19 and 29.' Michael McNamara, Clare's hurling trainer in 1995, when they won their first All-Ireland since 1914, and when they won their last All-Ireland in 1997. McNamara who is credited with being responsible for the legendary fitness of the Clare team refutes the claim that players are over stretched by the modern game.

'There is a notion in Armagh that we are bad for football in the county. That is nonsense. Armagh won nothing pre-Crossmaglen. If the other Armagh clubs are good enough on the day, let them beat us. If they are not, keep their mouths shut.' Donal Murtagh, Crossmaglen Rovers manager, refers to the clubs uninterrupted dominance of the Senior county championship since 1996, on this day in 2007.

March 17th

Footballer Jem Roche of Wexford who contested the world heavyweight boxing title on this day in 1908 and was knocked out in under three minutes went on to manage a multiple All-Ireland winning Wexford team.

'The first dagger is bad but the second dagger is even sorer into your heart. That's two years work out there, two years of graft, endless hours of planning and trying new ideas; it's soul-destroying at times.' Sean McLean the manager of Dunloy hurlers of Antrim on their second loss in a row in the All-Ireland Club final on this day in 2004. For six members of the Dunloy team it was the fourth loss in ten years.

Bray in Wicklow were the club chosen to represent Dublin in the 1902 All-Ireland football final under the old system of clubs representing the county.

March 18th

‘When I saw no one I got a bit of a fright. I said: am I gone mad or what. But you can’t blame the goalkeeper, he was going for the pass.’ Kieran Donaghy of Kerry discusses an open goal in the 2007 All-Ireland final.

From 1892 players could be selected from any county club to play in the inter-county championship, not just the club that had won the county championship. In truth this had been common practice with counties looking to put out the best sides in the hope of winning the All-Ireland and the new rule was a recognition of the practice.

Bill ‘Squires’ Gannon of Kildare was the first football captain to lift the Sam Maguire Cup in 1928 when they defeated Cavan 2-6 to 2-5.

March 19th

Eoin 'Bomber' Liston outscored the whole opposition team by two points when he scored 3-2 in the 1978 All-Ireland Senior football final against Dublin with the final score for the game 5-11 to 0-9. He won further All-Irelands in 1979, 1980, 1981, 1984, 1985 and 1986.

Dan Spring, the father of future leader of the Labour Party and Tánaiste Dick Spring, scored a goal in the All-Ireland Senior football final in 1939 to help the Kingdom to beat Meath 2-5 to 2-3. It would be the first of three titles in a row for Kerry.

'I'm just delighted we have another day. We actually get to hurl in June.' Dublin hurling manager Michael O'Grady on getting a draw with Laois in the 2000 championship.

March 20th

‘No inducement of any kind, financial or otherwise, was offered to DJ Carey to return to the game.’ Kilkenny County Board vice-chairman Ned Quinn on this day in 1998 when DJ Carey announced he would not retire after all.

Donegal are known as the men from Tir Chonnaill, The Hills, O’Donnell county, or the Herring gutters and won their first and only All-Ireland Senior football final in 1992.

‘In terms of on-the-field discipline, there is no doubt now that in relation to, probably more so football than hurling but I wouldn’t exclude hurling either, that teams are being coached to work to the very edge of the disciplinary rules.’ Nicky Brennan the GAA President speaking in 2008 on proposals to deal with persistent fouling.

March 21st

Antrim hurler Eddie Donnelly who played with the county for almost twenty years retired in 1985. In that time he won an All-Ireland Intermediate medal, was picked as a replacement All Star twice in the 70s, was named as full forward in the Antrim Team of the Century in 1984 and won eight Senior county championship medals with his club Ballycastle, three in a row between 1978 and 1980.

Carrying the ball on the hurley is first allowed in the GAA in 1895.

'If you are able to put a description on that, fair play to ye! With a quarter of an hour to go Tipperary would have been expected to win by just about everybody. Except, of course, ourselves!' Brian Cody the Kilkenny hurling manager on winning the National League final against Tipperary in 2003, 5-14 to 5-13. Kilkenny scored 4-4 out of 6-6 scored in the last fifteen minutes.

March 22nd

'It is disheartening that lack of discipline is an issue, almost on an annual basis, despite repeated warnings, suggestions and campaigns. Until the whole Association is prepared to accept that this is a major problem, there seems to be little point in making suggestions or stating the obvious.' GAA Director-General, Liam Mulvihill on this day in 2003.

A total of 237,377 spectators watch Dublin and Meath play four games in the 1991 first round of the Senior football Championship at Croke Park.

In 2008 the Mayo county board were given a €5,000 fine as a result of missiles being thrown from the crowd at Kerry players during a National League football game in Castlebar. Kerry players had coins and missiles thrown in their direction and the Mayo board was also instructed to install CCTV cameras at McHale Park to prevent any such thing happening again.

March 23rd

Croke Park was formerly the City and Suburban Grounds owned by Mr. Maurice Butterley

In 1918 British soldiers baton charged matches, in Offaly and Down, took down goal posts in Kildare and occupied grounds, in Cork and Cavan, to prevent games being played without a permit. The GAA responded by organising 2,000 matches to be played at the same time across the country. This brought to an end the new permit requirement that had been brought in to control public gatherings.

The Ban also known as Rule 27 was introduced in 1902 and banned GAA members from playing, attending or promoting soccer, rugby, hockey or cricket and remained in force until 1971. In 1938 Dr. Douglas Hyde, President of Ireland, had been removed under the ban as patron of the GAA for attending a soccer match.

March 24th

The first ever draw in an All-Ireland Senior football final is played on this day in 1895 for the delayed 1894 title, delayed finishes were common for the first thirty years of the All-Ireland championship. Dublin drew with Cork 0-6 to 1-1, the Cork goal was worth five points under the old rules. In a controversial replay Dublin were awarded the title when Cork left the field of play after several spectator incursions and refused to play on.

On this day in 1895 Cork become the first team to win the All-Ireland Senior hurling title three times in a row when they won the delayed 1894 Championship final against Dublin 5-20 to 2-0. Only four teams had competed in the championship with Dublin reaching the final without ever playing a game.

The first ever soccer match is played at Croke Park between Ireland and Wales on this day in 2007. Ireland win 1-0.

March 25th

The legendary Tubberadora hurling club represented Tipperary for the last time, in the All-Ireland final, on this day in 1898. The club went out of existence after winning their fourth All-Ireland Senior hurling title. Mike Maher scored three of their seven goals to beat Kilkenny 7-13 to 3-10. Kilkenny were appearing for the fourth time in a final and while they were becoming a force in hurling they had yet to win a title.

Limerick having lost both the National League hurling final and All-Ireland final in 1933 redeemed themselves in style by firstly winning the National League final on this day in 1934 and then winning the All-Ireland final in the same year. Both finals were played against Dublin and while the All-Ireland went to a replay Limerick won the league final 3-6 to 3-3 at the first time of asking.

Points were first introduced into Gaelic Games in 1888 to deal with the problem of scoreless draws.

March 26th

Cork won their second All-Ireland hurling title on this day in 1893 when they played Dublin for the delayed 1892 championship. This was the first final played by seventeen-a-side, previously twenty-one was the norm. Cork were awarded the title when Dublin walked off the pitch after fifty minutes. Cork represented by Redmonds had scored 2-4 while Dublin represented by Flag-Davitts scored 1-1 before the game ended, the Cork side contained several Blackrock players as was now officially sanctioned by the GAA and began a long association with the competition. Only three counties had entered into the All-Ireland hurling championship that year.

Dublin won their second All-Ireland Senior football title in a row on this day in 1893 playing, as was common in the early years, for the 1892 championship. They beat Kerry, represented by Laune Rangers, 1-4 to 0-3 in the first seventeen-a-side final previously twenty-one-a-side had been the norm. This was Kerry's first appearance in a football final and they would not appear again for another eleven years.

March 27th

Tipperary won their second title in a row, on this day in 1898, when they played in the delayed 1896 All-Ireland Senior hurling final. Played at Jones' Road, in front of around 3,500 spectators, at half time Tipperary were 4-6 to 0-1 in the lead. Dublin never recoverd, scoring only three points in the second half to lose 8-14 to 0-4. At that time a goal was worth five points!

'But I suppose it's delivering a message and the message is that, if you re a sub, you stay in the dugout until you're called on to the pitch.' Brendan Ward, Offaly County Board Chairman, speaking on this day in 1997 on suspensions handed down to two Under-21 footballers, even though they were not involved in the mass brawl that had broken out with the Dublin opposition. They had left the subs bench to help an injured team member

Wrestling and handgrips are banned from Gaelic games in 1888.

March 28th

Tipperary hurlers were expelled from the 1938 Munster Championship for fielding a player who had attended a rugby international.

The separate posts for scoring points that sat twenty-one yards either side of the goals in Gaelic games are abolished in 1907 and replaced with the now familiar Gaelic goal posts leading to a need for more accurate kicking for point scoring.

'We were fortunate to have a man in the right place at the right time who had the vision to create a future vista for Croke Park unknown as a concept in these islands.' Seán McCague, President of the GAA, praises the vision of Liam Mulvihill in bringing about the redevelopment of Croke Park, at the official opening of the 'New Hogan Stand' and 'Canal Ends' on this day in 2003.

March 29th

'I believe in tough physical football, but I always said that the referee's position is sacrosanct, that they are beyond reproach. What I did yesterday I cannot understand.' Wexford football manager JJ Barrett, speaking on this day in 1999, announcing his resignation after striking a referee. Barrett immediately apologised and resigned the next day. The incident came at the end of a National League game against Cavan where a late penalty gave the Breffni side victory. Barrett was later suspended for two years by the Games Administration Committee.

Down play at Páirc Esler, Newry with a capacity of 15,000.

Laune Rangers of Kerry who were founded in 1888 took their name from a group of bailiff landlords who operated in the area in the mid 1800s. They won their first Senior county championship in 1889. In 1996, they were crowned All-Ireland club champions.

March 30th

Cork, in a warm up for the All-Ireland final meeting against the same opposition later in the year, beat Dublin on this day in 1941 in the National League final at the Cork Athletic Grounds 4-11 to 2-7. Cork with players like Ted O'Sullivan, Christy Ring and Jack Lynch would win the first of four All-Ireland Senior titles in a row that year, Dublin would be on the receiving end for three of those All-Ireland finals.

'Not bad lads, eh? Not bad for a team who can't play, can't shoot and can't tackle!' Cork football selector John Corcoran after their All-Ireland semi-final defeat of Meath in 2007. Cork Senior football titles: 1890, 1911, 1945, 1973, 1989, 1990.

'To be honest I wouldn't be surprised at anything that would happen you dealing with Croke Park, I'm not going to get it and that's that.' Mick O'Dwyer on being passed over again for the Ireland manager's position, for the International Rules, on this day in 2005.

March 31st

‘Although we have not achieved or played in the manner that may be expected, it should be noted that the management team were extremely courageous in taking control at a point when Roscommon football was experiencing difficult times, and considering this, nothing can be taken away from the track records of the people involved.’ Roscommon County Board accepts the resignation of John Maughan as football manager on this day in 2008. Maughan was previously in charge of three Mayo Senior football teams that made it to the All-Ireland finals but lost on each occasion. The resignation came after a series of poor results in the National League and after three years at the helm.

‘I know if there wasn’t football in Offaly we’d be just as strong. Tipperary, Galway and Wexford would be the same. It gives them a very big advantage to be able to concentrate on one game.’ Brian Whelehan former Offaly player on the strength of Kilkenny hurling.

April 1st

The first All-Ireland Senior hurling final was held in Pat White's Field in Birr on this day, Easter Sunday, in 1888 between Tipperary and Galway. Tipperary captained by Jim Stapleton won the game 1-1 to 0-0. Tipperary were represented by Thurles and Galway by Meelick.

Kevin Fennelly former Kilkenny hurling manager was one of the famous Ballyhale family who played with the Shamrocks club when they won nine Kilkenny Senior championships and three All-Ireland club titles. He won three Senior All-Irelands with Kilkenny, two at under-21 level and two as a Minor.

'The damage done to GAA grounds in both Drogheda and Limerick was outlined in detail to a shocked audience, who had forgotten some of the worst aspects of Cromwellian conquest.' Kevin Myers 'report' on the motion to remove Rule 21.

April 2nd

Charlie Redmond won All-Ireland Senior football medals with Dublin in 1983 and 1995. He played his club football with Erin's Isle but also won a county championship hurling medal with Erin's Isle in 1983.

'What is this about Kildare forwards, the sheep in Connemara know this about them, passing tourists in Kildare can shout out the window at people, you can't score. Why is this?' Pat Spillane.

'The Dublin county board, team management and the individual involved have personally apologised to Thomas Freeman and regret that the incident ever occurred.' Response in 2008 from the Dublin county board to a complaint from Monaghan that 2007 All Star Thomas Freeman was head-butted by a member of the Dublin management team at the end of a drawn National League game between the sides.

April 3rd

'I was getting media calls non-stop before last year's Munster final and while it goes with the territory when you're a manager, players should not have to cope with those sort of demands all the time. It can be very draining.' Eamonn Cregan former Limerick manager on the distraction of the media.

Teams are reduced from twenty-one to seventeen in 1892 and a goal no longer outscores any number of points and is set equal to five points.

'You know, when we in Armagh had no pitch, we availed for many years of the kindness of the Armagh rugby club. That we can't return that seems almost an embarrassment.' Jarlath Burns, the former Armagh football captain, speaking about Rule 42 on this day in 2001.

April 4th

‘There’s a lot of football to be played before the end of the year. The only time you can talk about All-Irelands is when you get to the final.’ Conor Mortimer.

‘I’m not denigrating Gaelic football but hurling is different completely.’ Donal O’Grady former Cork manager.

‘We trained bloody hard in our day, I can tell you. Kevin Heffernan brought in all these new ideas. I know we were the first to start training on a Saturday morning, the day before matches. I know Mick O’Dwyer copied that. Of course we thought Heffo was gone mad.’ Jimmy Keaveney former Dublin footballer.

In a dedication ceremony in Croke Park on this day in 2006 the ‘Canal End’ is renamed in honour of Maurice Davin the first President of the GAA. Known henceforth as the Davin Stand.

April 5th

Limerick picked up another double in 1936 winning both the National League hurling title and the All-Ireland as they had two years previously. The league final was again played against Dublin with Mick Mackay scoring the first goal for Limerick in a high scoring, 7-2 to 4-4, victory on this day in 1936 to give them their third league success in a row.

After the crowd invaded the field four times in the 1939 Ulster Senior football final the referee finally called the game off. The final incident occurred when the Armagh captain, Jim McCullough, was punched by a spectator while taking a sideline free.

'The arrogant, warmongering words of God Save the Queen ringing out over Croke Park is surely pushing the boundaries of tolerance and common sense beyond what is expected in any republic on earth.' JJ Barrett of Kerry offers a dissenting voice on England's visit to Croke Park.

April 6th

‘Dublin on top is good for the game generally. The game will always benefit when there is a strong Dublin team because everybody wants to beat us.’ Former Dublin footballer Charlie Redmond.

‘A small rump of malcontents.’ Dessie Farrell of Dublin on an anti-grant meeting in Toome, Co Antrim.

‘I am very pleased indeed to be able to inform you now of the details of the Government’s further generous commitment to our association. They have committed a total of £45,000,000 to Croke Park over the next three years and have pledged a further £15,000,000 for the necessary work to the northern end to render it ready and suitable to host the opening ceremony of the Special Olympics in 2003.’ Seán McCague, GAA President, in his surprise opening address to the annual Congress on this day in 2001.

April 7th

In a year of atrocious weather that saw a series of National football league games cancelled by firstly snow blizzards and then heavy rain it was decided to pick the four teams that lead the division to play off for the final in 1947. The final played on this day in 1947 was won by Derry who beat Clare 2-9 to 2-5 for their first National League title, a feat they would not repeat until 1992.

Monaghan win their first National league final on this day in 1985 when they beat Armagh, 1-11 to 0-9, with Eamonn McEneaney scoring Mongahan's only goal from a penalty.

'I firmly believe that the whole question of the role of the GAA president and the demands being made upon him will necessitate a review of the question of making the post full time.' Joe McDonagh former president of the GAA.

April 8th

For the third time Dublin win two All-Ireland Senior football finals in a row on this day in 1900, playing for the delayed 1898 championship. Dublin, represented by Geraldines, beat Waterford, represented by Erin's Hope, with two goals from Joe Ledwidge to win 2-8 to 0-4.

'The next time we play it will not be a pleasant sight.' Liam McHale commenting on his sending off against Meath in the 1996 All-Ireland Senior football final.

Roscommon play at Dr. Hyde Park with a capacity of 28,000.

'After Thurles we may look upon the GAA as a purely Fenian Society.' Special Branch Report after the IRB had taken control of the GAA in 1888.

April 9th

'It was a road we did not want to travel but today we could feel vindication that we did. It caused major upset and major division among the GAA community but it focused minds.' Dessie Farell GPA CEO comments on the government grant agreement and the player's threat to strike.

Derry appear in their first ever All-Ireland final in 1958 but were beaten by Dublin 2-12 to 1-9. Derry had reached the final with a sensational win over Kerry in the semi-final when Seán O'Connell scored a shock goal in the last two minutes of the game against the Kingdom.

'It is killing us and you're the b****cks that's to blame.' Clare hurling trainer Michael McNamara recounts a story of a man he met at a wedding blaming him for the intense training he now has to endure with his local team because of the success of McNamara's similar training regime with the 1995 and the 1997 All-Ireland Champions.

April 10th

‘We thought that was a reasonable, practical and courteous thing to do, so I issued the letters on that basis.’ Bertie Ahern, An Taoiseach, explains the offer of £60,000,000 to support the redevelopment of Croke Park was sent to the GAA before informing the partners in government because it was a fair reflection of discussions held at that stage and the GAA was keen to inform members at their Annual Congress. Speaking to the Dáil on this day in 2001.

A Standard Corporate box in Croke Park costs €240,000 while a top of the range Super box costs €450,000.

‘Referees, who it must be recalled are also human, are forced to watch and control actors, cheats, divers, liars and an ever-decreasing proportion of honorable men.’ Liam Griffen Wexford Hurling manager April 2003.

April 11th

Mayo picked up another National League football title on this day in 1949, their eighth, when they beat Louth 1-8 to 1-6 at Croke Park in front of 28,342 spectators.

Dublin are most often referred to as the Dubs but also answer to the Blues, the Metropolitans, the Jackeens or the Liffeysiders. They have twenty-two Senior football titles and six Senior hurling titles.

'It was an unprecedented situation. Usually the referee is the only person with the power to call off a game.' GAA PRO Danny Lynch on a Garda taking the names of players and advising the abandonment of a Minor hurling fixture in Kilmallock, Co Limerick in 1999 when a free for all broke out on the pitch and the Garda, who had arrived to watch the end of the game, had to intervene.

April 12th

GAA delegates agree on this day in 2008 the €3.5 million package proposed by the Minister for Arts, Sport and Tourism, to recognise the contribution of Senior inter-county GAA players.

'As long as the red jersey of Cork and the blue of Munster and the green black and gold of Glen Rovers, colours that Christy wore with such distinction, as long as we see these colours in manly combat the memories of Christy's genius and prowess will come tumbling back with profusion.' Jack Lynch at Christy Ring's funeral.

Arthur Bell Nicholls, husband of Charlotte Bronte, helped to found 'The Harp and Banagher' GAA football club in Offaly, at the beginning of the Association and revival in Gaelic games, in 1884.

April 13th

Prior to the 1798 Rebellion it was very common for the landed classes to support, referee and even play Gaelic games. Large sums of money were wagered and prizes offered up for the winning team with alcoholic refreshment laid on. The ferocity and at times sectarian nature of the '98 Rebellion created a hardening of attitudes and hard times in general saw the games go into serious decline in the early part of the nineteenth century. The first real signs of revival were the unlikely source of Trinity College Dublin where a hurley club was established to resurrect the game in the 1850s.

'Clogherhead Dreadnoughts, the only club banned for life from playing GAA. Twice.' Brendán Ó hEither in the Sunday Tribune 1982

A goal in Gaelic sports is set to three points in 1896 and has remained the same ever since.

April 14th

Kilkenny and Cork played in the delayed 1905 All-Ireland Senior hurling final on this day in 1907. While Cork won the game 5-10 to 3-13, objections by Kilkenny and then Cork compelled the GAA Central Council to order a replay. Kilkenny objected on the grounds that the Cork goalkeeper was a British army reservist and banned under Rule 21. Cork raised a counter objection that a Kilkenny player had already played for Waterford in the same championship. Kilkenny won the replay to win their second All-Ireland title.

'Modus operandi of seducing one of the G.A.A. into the I.R.B society.' Title of a a Special Branch report on this day in 1890 giving an outline of the methods of the IRB for seducing GAA members into the ranks of the republican cause. Luckily part of the test is to give the candidate lots of drink to see if he will 'blab' under the influence.

April 15th

Though hotly disputed by many it is claimed that the character of the Citizen, a bigoted nationalist and anti Semite, in James Joyce's Ulysses was based on Michael Cusack. While the ban on Royal Irish Constabulary is a feature of the early GAA there is no evidence Cusack supported it and in fact had such a rule over turned while a member of the Dublin Athletics club. One of his biggest criticisms of other organisations was that they were too nationalist and his main drive appears to have been the preservation of Irish pastimes under the control of an Irish organisation.

Dublin play at Parnell Park with a capacity of 12,000.

'An integral part of the organisation's efforts to communicate with its members here in Ireland and throughout the world.' Joe McDonagh, President of the GAA officially launches their web site on this day in 1999.

April 16th

Nemo Rangers of Cork, who have produced such greats as Billy Morgan and Colin Corkery, appeared in their eighth All-Ireland club final on this day in 2001 having lost only one of their previous appearances. This would be a second loss for the club when they were beaten 0-16 to 1-12 by Crossmolina Deel Rovers, however they would be back again to reclaim the title in 2002 for the seventh time.

The first Sam Maguire cup was awarded in the 1928 All-Ireland Senior football final and was replaced with a newer model in 1988.

'Nicky Brennan and his committee have put a muzzle on us.' Babs Keating on being asked to comment on the referee in 2007.

April 17th

Christy Ring played forty-four times in the Railway Cup scoring forty-two goals and one-hundred-and-four points, he was on the winning team eighteen times.

The 1980 All-Ireland club hurling final was know as the 'Connolly Donnelly' final because the Castlegar team from Galway had five Connollys and the Ballycastle team from Antrim had six Donnellys hurling for them. Castlegar won the game 1-11 to 1-8.

Pierce Grace won three Senior All-Irelands with the Kilkenny Hurlers 1911-13 and two Senior football All-Irelands with Dublin 1906-07.

'Maybe it is a reflection of Irish society today.' Nicky Brennan reflects on the discipline issue in the GAA.

April 18th

Limerick scored eleven goals against Cork on this day in 1937 to win their fourth National League title in a row. In a game that saw two greats of the game face up to each other as captains, Jack Lynch for Cork and Mick Mackey for Limerick, the Treaty county were too much for Cork winning 11-6 to 5-1.

Gaelic teams are reduced from seventeen players to fifteen in 1913.

'A fan is someone who, if you have made an idiot of yourself on the pitch, doesn't think you've done a permanent job.' Jack Lynch

'A good win – forty-three, forty-four years waiting for this I think, but we got it in the end.' Dan Shanahan the Waterford hurler speaking in 2007 after they beat Kilkenny to win their first National League title since 1963.

April 19th

Mayo footballers are beaten by Meath in the final game of the National League on this day in 1936 but still win their second National League title having gone into the final game four points clear.

'Cumann Luthcleas Gael pledges its intent to delete Rule 21 from its official guide when effective steps are taken to implement the amended structures and policing arrangements envisaged in the British-Irish peace agreement.' Rule 21 remains May 1998.

'I believe that we must show vision, courage, leadership and unity and not stand idly by.' GAA president Joe McDonagh calls a special congress in 1998 to debate deleting Rule 21.

'Players are training to get past the first round, not training to win a Leinster final.' Cyril Hughes former Carlow manager.

April 20th

‘It’s not what we wanted to see but there was a great game of football played also.’ Paul Caffrey former Dublin football manager speaking after a win over Meath confirmed their promotion to Division One but saw five players sent off in the first half on this day in 2008. The game which saw a twenty-nine player bust up resulted in sixteen players receiving suspensions, eight from each, and a €20,000 fine for each county. Meath had their fine reduced to €10,000 on appeal.

Fermanagah are known as the Ernersiders, Lakeland county or Maguire county and have yet to win a Senior title having won one All-Ireland in Junior football.

‘What I really want to see wiped out is that awful psychological barrier, where Dublin players would start shivering when they came up against the black and amber.’ Tom Fitzpatrick manager of the Dublin under-sixteen hurlers in 2000.

April 21st

In a replay of the 1894 All-Ireland Senior football championship in Thurles on this day in 1895 Cork are leading the game when Dublin withdraw from the field of play. This follows a general melee when members of the Dublin team are attacked by supporters invading the pitch in the final minutes of the game. Central council awards the game to Dublin, effectively disqualifying Cork who withdrew from the association for a year in protest.

'I can't understand why a player should go through that kind of pressure and such a long journey in the space of twenty-four hours.' Armagh footballer Diarmuid Marsden on having to play a National League game on a Saturday then for Ulster on the Sunday, adding insult he was injured in the Sunday game.

Tackling the goalkeeper in the parallelogram is banned in 1975.

April 22nd

'The training ground has to be a place of opportunity. Everyone has to fight for their place; no one owns the jersey.' Brian Cody the Kilkenny manager.

'It was very humiliating for me and the lads,' Tommy Dowd on posing for pictures with the Sam Maguire Cup in the forecourt at the entrance to the new Cusack Stand, at a reception for the winners of the All-Ireland in 1996, but being refused admission because he had not got an official ticket of invitation. He was still carrying the cup.

'I plead with you to give your backing to the players. They voted unanimously to back the move 100 per cent. I am asking you to do the same.' Captain of the Galway hurlers David Collins asks the County Board to support the move to the Leinster championship in 2009. The Board voted in favour.

April 23rd

Glen Rovers in Cork won county Senior hurling honours eight times in a row between 1934 and 1941. The club was to form the backbone of the famous four-in-a-row Cork side featuring Jack Lynch and Christy Ring among many greats from the club. They won their first All-Ireland Senior club title in 1973 when they beat St. Rynagh's of Offaly, 2-18 to 2-8.

Kerry withdrew from the 1917 championship due to the number of GAA members who had been interned after the 1916 rising.

'If you asked them to shorten a hurley they'd probably start at the wrong end.' Babs Keating former Tipperary manager on the media.

April 24th

Longford were well on their way to a first National league football title when they beat the reigning All-Ireland and National League champions Galway in the home final on this day in 1966, 0-9 to 0-8. Longford captained by Brendan Barden went on to beat New York for the title proper over two games at the start of October. By that time Galway had recovered from their defeat to lift the Sam Maguire cup for the third year in a row.

'I know of the trauma and outrage caused by the violation to our properties and the occupation of Crossmaglen. But we cannot dwell on the past.' Joe McDonagh, President of the GAA, on this day in 1998.

'Of course it was disappointing to lose those All-Ireland finals but I still got up the next day and carried on. I still had a life to lead. I love football, I don't just like it. You can't just like it.' John Maughan former Mayo manager.

April 25th

Tipperary played Dublin in the 1908 All-Ireland hurling final on this day in 1909. Dublin represented by Kickams rallied with a late goal to earn a draw, 2-5 to 1-8, against Tipperary represented by Thurles. Tipperary went on to win the replay to earn their eighth title.

'I don't expect it to be open, I don't expect it to be attractive. As we know Ulster teams tend to have a negative influence on Gaelic football in general.' Colm O'Rourke.

'At peak viewing times, RTE reported 879,000 viewers for the hurling final and 795,000 for the football decider. Average viewing figures for the afternoon were 584,000 and 552,000 respectively, peaking during the actual matches.' Official viewing figures released by RTE in 1996. The hurling final had seen two outsiders playing, Wexford beat Limerick 1-13 to 0-14, while the football had been a drawn game between Meath and Mayo.

April 26th

Dublin won their first National League final on this day in 1953 when under the captaincy of Maurice Whelan and with a team that contained Footballer of the Millennium Kevin Heffernan they beat the reigning All-Ireland champions Cavan. Heffernan scored 2-2 to help his side to a 4-6 to 0-9 victory.

Kerry won the delayed 1924 All-Ireland Senior football title to deprive Dublin of four-in-a-row titles on this day in 1925. Con Brosnan of the Kingdom kicked a last minute free to win the game 0-4 to 0-3.

Bryan Smyth was the first Meath player to lift the Sam Maguire Cup when they won their first Senior football title in 1949. Meath Senior football titles: 1949, 1954, 1967, 1987, 1988, 1996, 1999.

April 27th

Austin Stack who captained Kerry to their second All-Ireland Senior football title in 1904 died on this day in 1929. A member of the IRB he was involved heavily in the planning of the 1916 rising and an opponent of the treaty. He died due to health severely weakened by a forty-one day hunger strike while a prisoner during the civil war. He had previously won an All-Ireland in 1903 also.

Mayo, having missed out in the 1940 National League football campaign to end their six-in-a-row, were back on winning ways when they won the final on this day in 1941. They beat Dublin, 3-5 to 0-7, with Josie Munnelly from Castlebar getting two of the Mayo goals and Peter Laffey getting the third.

'I was amazed because there was an actual injury in injury-time.' Former Galway manager John O'Mahony comments on the mystery of injury time in their National League defeat to Kerry in 2004.

April 28th

Limerick playing in the National League final on this day in 1938 faced the reigning All-Ireland Champions Tipperary to set a record of five league titles in a row. Limerick captained again by Mick Mackay were convincing winners 5-2 to 1-1 in a game which saw Tipperary fail to register a single score in the first half.

'I used feel after all matches fierce anti-climactic. You're on a high for a minute or two before everything falls back into proportion and after that the euphoria slips back. A minute before, you're almost crying wondering if you're going to win. Then the whistle goes and you wonder what's it all about.' Dinny Allen Cork captain of the All-Ireland Senior football champions in 1989.

'The more used you get to playing Croke Park the worse it gets.' Páidí Ó Sé.

April 29th

On this day in 1888 the first All-Ireland Senior Football final was played at Clonskeagh between Limerick and Louth. Limerick captained by Denis Corbett won the first All-Ireland Senior football title 1-4 to 0-3.

Kerry win their first ever National League football final when they beat Kildare on this day in 1928.

Dennis Taylor who won the World Snooker Championship in the early hours of this day in 1985 played Minor football for Tyrone.

'I just can't wait to wake up in the morning and know that I've won. I have a National league title in my pocket. I wasn't going to be a loser my whole life in football but if I hadn't won something then I would have been.' Mayo footballer David Brady after they beat Galway in the National League final on this day in 2001.

April 30th

Waterford faced Dublin in Thurles on this day in 1939 for the National League hurling final having lost to the Blues in the previous year's All-Ireland final. Once again Dublin were too strong and won the game 1-8 to 1-4 leaving Waterford to wait another twenty-four years to win a National League title.

Galway are known as the Tribesmen and won their first All-Ireland Senior hurling final in 1923 and their first football final in 1934 adding four and nine titles in each code since. No All-Ireland Senior football final was played in 1925 but the title was awarded to Galway as Connacht champions. Galway Senior football titles: 1925, 1934, 1938, 1956, 1964, 1965, 1966, 1998, 2001.

'Let's f★★★★★g hold a tight rein here.' Referee Pat McEnaney to his fellow officials at half time in a GAA match in 1999 as shown in an RTÉ documentary 'Blowing the Whistle.'

May 1st

Knockmore of Mayo were only founded in 1957. In their first year playing Senior football they were crowned county champions in 1973 and became the first Mayo club to win the Connacht club championship. In 1996 they won their second Connacht club title but were defeated by Crossmaglen Rangers in the All-Ireland club final.

'We fully support the actions of the hurlers and confirm that accordingly we are withdrawing our services until further notice.' Statement from the Cork football panel in 2002 joining the hurlers on strike.

'I've been saying all along that this was a very important title for us to win.' Joe Kernan, the Armagh manager who played on the losing Armagh side in the 1985 final, speaking after Armagh won their first National League football title on this day in 2005. They beat Wexford, 1-21 to 1-14, who were appearing in the final for the first time since 1946. Steven McDonnell's 0-10 added to Armagh's very convincing win.

May 2nd

‘It was nice, d’you know, we’ve had a lot of bad days up here in these dressing rooms in the last couple of years.’ Kerry footballer, Johnny Crowley, who scored two goals on this day in 2004 to give Kerry their sixteenth National League title.

Fermanagh play at Brewster Park, Enniskillen.

In 1999 camogie moved from a twelve a side a game to a fifteen a side game.

‘If there was ever a group of people worthy of a psychological study, it is surely the men who have donned the Kildare football jersey over the past 40 years.’ Eugene McGee in a preview of Kildare’s Senior football championship replay match against Dublin in 1998, Kildare won and went on to lose the All-Ireland final to Galway.

May 3rd

Offaly appeared in their first National League final on this day in 1981 where they were beaten by a Cork side who scored two goals within three minutes of the start, Jimmy Barry Murphy getting the second after Tim Crowley scored the first. Offaly scored only once in the first half with a goal from Pádraig Horan but made up some ground in the second half losing 3-11 to 2-8.

Dublin footballers win the home final of the National League on this day in 1964 when they beat Down, 2-9 to 0-7. Despite being the reigning All-Ireland champions they would be beaten by New York in the away final.

'For a number of years, I have been warning that the attitude towards discipline was less than satisfactory and this year was proof positive that there is a major problem at every level of the Association.' Liam Mulvihill former GAA Director-General speaking in 2005.

May 4th

'Never in the history of outdoor games in Ireland have people gone home so well pleased with what they saw.' Dick 'Dickeen' FitzGerald on the first fifteen-a-side game in Gaelic football played between Louth and Kerry on this day in 1913 when the two sides met in the final of the Croke Cup. 25,000 spectators turned up to see who might have won between the two sides had Kerry not stood down from the 1910 All-Ireland final between the two, over a dispute with a rail company. The game ended in a draw 1-1 to 0-4.

In 1893 the reigning All-Ireland football champions Dublin declined to take part in the Senior football Championship, Wexford went on to win that year

'It's fantastic. It didn't go for me on the day, but luckily it went for the team.' DJ Carey on only scoring one point from play in the 1993 All-Ireland Senior hurling final but Kikenny still beat Galway 2-17 to 1-15. He is named the Texaco Hurler of the Year for 1993.

May 5th

Kildare appeared in their fifth National League football final on this day in 1991. They had never won a final previously and this final would be no different with Dublin's Vinny Murphy scoring the goal that separated the sides, 1-9 to 0-10.

'We have a serious problem with discipline. During the past year we had to set up four separate investigations arising out of serious incidents that had taken place at our games.' Donegal Secretary Noreen Doherty in 2005.

Prior to 2001 Westmeath hadn't picked up a single All Star, that year footballer Rory O'Connor picked up their first.

'I hope the foxes are plentiful in the next world and I have six good beagles when we move on to the great hunting ground in the sky.' Ger Loughnane hopes there is more to the next life than just hurling.

May 6th

Wexford beat Tipperary in a National League hurling decider on this day in 1956. The Slaneysiders had been down fifteen points at half time 2-10 to 0-1. After the restart Nicky Rackard scored a goal to put Wexford on their way to an amazing recovery and National League title with a final score of 5-9 to 2-14.

'Michael McGoldrick put Conor Mortimer in his pocket and fed him on farts.' Joe Brolly calls it as he sees it in novel fashion.

Limerick were the first to lift the Liam McCarthy Cup in 1923 when they beat Dublin in a replayed final. The cup was named in honour of the previous President and Secretary of the London County Board.

May 7th

All-Ireland Senior football champions Meath were held to a, 1-12 to 1-12, draw in the National League football final against Derry on this day in 2000 when Trevor Giles scored from an injury time free. Derry would go on to win their fifth title in the replay, 1-8 to 0-9.

The Ballyhale Shamrocks in Kilkenny were first formed in 1972 when two local clubs amalgamated but it was not long before they came to national prominence winning the All-Ireland club final in 1981, beating St. Finbarr's in Cork, 1-15 to 1-11. They had reached the club final two years earlier losing out to Blackrock of Cork. The club is closely associated with the Fennelly family of seven brothers all of whom played Senior hurling for the county at different stages but has also turned out talented hurler Henry Shefflin.

'The worst thing about the game was there wasn't even a chance of a row.' Colm O'Rourke

May 8th

For the first time two Ulster teams faced off in the 1960 National league football final on this day when Down beat Cavan 0-12 to 0-9 in front of 49,451 spectators at Croke Park. Down would go on to win their first Senior All-Ireland in the same year repeating the success one year later in the championship and two years later in the league.

'It is all about the players one to thirty-four, who have been training together to put back-to-back titles together. It comes down to work-rate and attitude and honesty.'
Declan O'Sullivan the Kerry captain on what it takes to win two All-Irelands in a row.

'I swear to God, my mother would be faster than most of those three fellas and she has a bit of arthritis in the knee.'
Pat Spillane on the Armagh full back line at half time in the 2002 All-Ireland football final, they went on to win.

May 9th

Carlow made their first appearance in a National League football final on this day in 1954 but lost out to a very impressive Mayo who were lifting their ninth National League title with a final score of 2-10 to 0-3. Carlow only managed to score one point in the second half.

'They punished every mistake as they nearly always do.' Michael Bond the Offaly manager on Kilkenny.

'The feeling wasn't so much one of anger as devastation.' Carlow footballer Johnny Nevin on a controversial exit from the championship on this day in 1999 when four players from Carlow and two from Westmeath were sent off and the referee produced his book no less than twenty times to implement stricter discipline rules for the championship. Carlow appealed and the Leinster Council announced a replay, then Westmeath counter appealed and Central Council said the referee's decision was final and the original result was left to stand.

May 10th

Mayo won their tenth National League football title on this day in 1970 when they beat Down 4-7 to 0-10. Down missed a penalty, which was swiftly punished by the first of two Mayo goals scored by JJ Cribben. Mayo were the first county to attain ten titles and Kerry would not match the record until 1972 when they were into the second year of a four-in-a-row sweep only bettered by Mayo in the thirties.

Kerry are known as the Kingdom and have won thirty-four All-Ireland Senior football finals and a solitary All-Ireland Senior hurling final.

We'll circle the wagons and drive on, and that starts in the Horse and Jockey.' Babs Keating on how Tipperary would deal with defeat.

May 11th

'Kerry have learned the value of tackling and work-rate from the Ulster teams of the last few years. Remember the second half of the 2002 final when Armagh lifted their intensity and their tackling to another level? The same with Tyrone in 2003 and '05. Kerry have reacted by putting huge emphasis on that area of the game while still retaining the more traditional elements of their own style - quick movement of the ball and long delivery to the full forward line.' Jack O'Connor former Kerry manager explains what effect Ulster teams have had on the Kingdom.

Tipperary won their first All-Ireland Senior camogie final in 1999.

'Every week I'm getting more confident. The balls are just starting to kick and players are starting to kick the ball to me.' Setanta Ó hAilpín after two years in the AFL starts to get some passes.

May 12th

Seán Brown the Chairman of Ballaghy GAA Club was abducted, and later murdered by loyalist paramilitaries, as he locked up the GAA clubhouse after a committee meeting on this night in 1997.

Roscommon, playing Kerry, were ahead by three points in the National League football final as injury time ticked away on this day in 1974. Unfortunately the Rossies were unable to hold out for their first National League title when John Egan scored a late goal to force a replay. Two weeks later Kerry were more convincing by six points to win the title for the fourth year in a row.

'The old game of hurling has fallen so completely into oblivion that those appointed to procure hurls and balls discovered the art of manufacturing these articles was as extinct as the dodo. This difficulty is being got over, and early next week old Irish hurls will be on sale once more.' Michael Cusack, Irish Sportsman 1882.

May 13th

Offaly appeared in their first ever National League football home final on this day in 1969 but two goals and two points from Kerry forward Mick O'Dwyer, matching the Offaly team score, put paid to their hopes with the Kingdom winning 3-11 to 0-8. Both teams would meet again in the All-Ireland final later that year when the Kingdom won again but this time by three points. Kerry went on to win the National League title proper against New York by seven points over two legs.

'We make this acknowledgement because we are concerned that the story and pictures which were published in a Sunday newspaper have damaged the preparation of the Roscommon Senior football team for our crucial championship match against Galway next Sunday.' Statement released, by two Roscommon Senior county footballers, on this day in 2002 admitting they were the players who played a game of night time pool, in the nude, in a Derry hotel as reported in the Sunday People.

May 14th

Mayo won their sixth National League football title in a row on this day in 1939 when they took Meath on, in front of a home crowd of 10,000, winning the game 5-9 to 0-6 with two Paddy Moclair goals.

Five brothers, two Coughlans and three Ahernes, were on the Cork team that won the first National League hurling final on this day in 1926 beating Dublin 3-7 to 1-5. Michael, Paddy and David Aherne each scored a goal making their combined score higher than that scored by the whole Dublin team in the final. Cork won the All-Ireland Senior hurling final in the same year beating Kilkenny.

Dublin gain revenge for their loss in the 1919 All-Ireland Senior final when they beat the same opposition, Cork, 4-9 to 4-3, for the 1920 title. Even though the final is for 1920 the game is played two years later on this day in 1922, due to continuing fighting in the country.

May 15th

In the 1917 and 1921 Senior football championships Meath failed to score at all.

Brian Whelehan of the Birr club in Offaly was the only modern player to be listed on the Hurling Team of the Millennium when it was announced in 1999. He would not retire for another eight years and received the accolade a year after winning his second and last All-Ireland Senior medal in 1998. It was a game in which he was famously switched from defence to full forward in a week in which he had been suffering from the flu, he scored 1-6 to help his team best Kilkenny 2-16 to 1-13. He was named at left halfback on the Hurling Team of the Millennium.

The Dublin County board adopts a light blue jersey bearing the city arms as the county colours in 1913. Originally the shorts were white but changed to navy in 1974.

May 16th

Footballer Pat Reynolds was the first Meath man to be selected as an All-Star in 1971.

When Dublin won the 1927 All-Ireland Senior hurling final not a single member of the team was originally from Dublin, the introduction of the declaration rule allowing players to opt for their home county had a detrimental effect on Dublin hurling which had benefitted from those working in the capital. Having won five All-Irelands up to 1927 they have only won one more since.

'When you have experienced what it is like to win an All-Ireland once, you would hate to go through your career without doing it again.' Liam Dunne, Wexford hurler who was part of the winning All-Ireland side in 1996 when they beat Limerick, 1-14 to 0-13. Speaking on this day in 1999.

May 17th

Just prior to throw in for a game between Crossmaglen Rovers and Silverbridge, on this day in 1972, a British Army helicopter lands in the middle of the pitch and British army personnel proceed to clear the pitch leaving one Silverbridge player hospitalised. This would become a recurring pattern throughout the troubles, in 1972 British army helicopters landed on the pitch while games were being played on at least five separate occasions.

Dublin won ten All-Ireland Senior camogie finals between 1957 and 1966.

'Like the Nike advertisement says. Just Do It. That sums up what managers should say to teams. What people should say to themselves. Regardless of whether there is 50,000 there or nobody there. Just Do It.' Joe Brolly Derry footballer on managers advice to teams.

May 18th

Kevin Heffernan scored in the third minute of the 1958 National League football final to help Dublin on their way to a third title on this day beating Kildare 3-13 to 3-8. Dublin would go on to win the All-Ireland in the same year.

In 1927 Kildare won both the Leinster Senior football final and the All-Ireland final by the exact same 05-03 score line beating Dublin and Kerry respectively. Kildare Senior football titles 1905, 1919, 1927, and 1928.

Galway won their first All-Ireland Senior camogie title in 1996.

'Being beaten.' - Wexford captain Nigel Higgins when asked what his memories were of playing Kilkenny.

May 19th

'If I was with any other county team, the chances are that the manager would have let me go altogether, but Seán tries to keep a set panel for as long as he can. We've lived in each other's pockets for the last five years, become as much a family as a team. That helps because when the chips are down, everyone knows what everyone else is capable of doing.' Evan Kelly the Meath wing forward who in scoring three points from play in the 1999 All-Ireland Senior football final rewarded the manager Seán Boylan's decision to stick with him, three points was the difference in the score between Meath and Cork.

A report appears in the 'Dublin Courant' newspaper on this day in 1748 on a hurling match played between Munster and Leinster in which, the later were victorious and in a return game Leinster won again.

'Awesome - that's the only word to describe them.' Former Offaly manager Michael Bond describes Kilkenny hurlers.

May 20th

At the request of the DPP two students are found innocent, on this day in 2003, of breaking into Croke Park . Both had originally admitted climbing over the Jones' Road Gate and one had been in a state of undress on the pitch when gardaí arrived. The incident had happened the night before the All-Ireland Senior hurling final between Clare and Kilkenny in 2002.

When Birr in Offaly beat Dunloy of Antrim in the 2003 All-Ireland club championship final they became the first club to win the title four times. Considering they did not win their first title until 1995 it is a remarkable achievement brought on in great part by the close association of the Whelehan family with the club. Brian Whelehan is the only modern player to have been named on the Hurling Team of the Millennium. The club has also produced other great players such the Pilkington brothers and Joe Errity.

May 21st

Jack Lynch, the future Taoiseach, wins his sixth All-Ireland Senior medal in 1946 when Cork beat Kilkenny, 7-5 to 3-8, under the captaincy of his good friend Christy Ring. Five of those medals were in hurling while the other was for the All-Ireland Senior football title in 1945 when Cork beat Cavan 2-5 to 0-7.

'The Day we quit hurling is the day we all become 40 stone.' Satanta Ó hAilpín.

Galway won five Senior Connacht football finals in a row between 1956 and 1960.

'We went to college but we would have had no interest in books, we only went to university to play football,' Cathal O'Rourke of Armagh.

May 22nd

‘They weren’t dominating like the first half but they were still four points up and they looked like they were still in control but when the goal came, by Jesus it all disappeared. They seemed to die. You can look at everything else, but McConville’s goal changed the game. The moment he got the goal it all changed. A goal will lift a team no end.’ Mick O’Dwyer the former Kerry manager on what went wrong for Kerry in the 2002 All-Ireland Senior final when they were beaten, 1-12 to 0-14, by Armagh.

The Kilkenny hurler, DJ Carey, is also a notable handball player winning national titles on several occasions, in a doubles partnership with Michael Walsh.

‘But I always felt that he was truly an extraordinary hurler and from the start I marked the ten spot as “reserved for the God.”’ Mícheál Ó Muircheartaigh picks Christy Ring for his greatest hurling team selection.

May 23rd

'It is the greatest injustice of all time and we are devastated.' Tipperary Chairman Michael Frawley after their appeal for a replay against Kerry was turned down even though it was admitted a mistake had been made. Kerry had been awarded a goal in their championship football clash with Tipperary that television clearly showed had already gone wide on this day in 1999.

Galway play at Pearse Stadium, Salthill, Kenny Park, Athenry and St. Jarlath's, Tuam with capacities of 32,000, 13,000 and 28,000 each.

'Who wants to win an All-Ireland in a building site anyway?' Graham Geraghty the Meath captain, after Meath were eliminated from the 1998 Leinster Championship, referring to the redevelopment of Croke Park.

May 24th

Ballina Stephenites of Mayo were founded in 1886, and won their first county Senior title in 1889. Between 1904 and 1916 they won thirteen titles in a row. Between 1923 and 1929 they won seven county titles in a row. When Mayo won their first All-Ireland Senior title in 1936 the club supplied George Ormsby, Jackie Carney, Paddy Moclair and Gerard Corull to the team.

'Our game is a team game and teams must have game plans, several of them.' Seán Boylan former Meath manager.

'Every player in our team lifted themselves today. To watch it was unbelievable. At the end, with the crowd cheering the passes and us so far ahead, well, I don't know. You could never write a script for a game like that.' Galway captain Gary Fahey after his county won the All-Ireland football final by beating Meath 0-17 to 0-8 in 2001.

May 25th

‘Being a Kerry manager is probably the hardest job in the world because Kerry people, I’d say, are the roughest type of f**king animals you could ever deal with. And you can print that.’ Páidí Ó Sé.

JJ Kilmartin the Kilkenny handball player won seven hardball titles before breaking his neck in a road accident, he returned to the game to win three titles in a row between 1930 and 1937.

‘In certain minds, it’s always chains and ashes. Especially in places like Wexford and Clare."Jaysus, boy, we dragged tractors through bogs." It’s a load of nonsense. You wouldn’t win an All-Ireland doing that.’ Liam Griffin, Wexford hurling manager.

May 26th

Seán O'Neill of Down scored a goal to help his team to their third National League football title against Kildare on this day in 1968. Despite two goals from Tommy Carew the Lilywhites could not overcome the Mourne men to win their first ever National League title. Down would add an All-Ireland Senior football title to their list of honours by the end of the year when they beat Kerry, O'Neill would score another goal on that day too.

'Surreptitious advertising - which has become increasingly of concern in the recent past - is prohibited under Irish law and EU Law. Where intended breaches are brought to RTÉ's attention, RTÉ Television has no choice but to implement the guidelines under which it must operate.' RTÉ justifies banning players advertising products during post match interviews and the subsequent criticism by the GPA on this day in 2005.

May 27th

'It was a goal outstanding players score when their back's against the wall.' Brian Cody describes a goal by DJ Carey.

Ollie Crinnigan was the first Kildare footballer to win an All Star in 1978.

In 1999 camogie moved from a twelve-a-side a game to a fifteen a-side-game.

'I came up from Limerick with a few of the selectors and the trainer and when we got to Mullingar only seven of the sixty-one turned up. And two of those were injured.' Tom Ryan on his resignation from the manager's position with the Westmeath hurlers in November 2004.

May 28th

Maurice Davin's resignation as the first President of the GAA is accepted at a convention in Limerick on this day in 1887. He had survived just long enough to see both the first hurling and the football championships be completed. Three years after the start of the association two of its key members are no longer in controlling positions, Cusack had been dismissed in July of the previous year having fallen out with Archbishop Croke.

Kildare are known as the Lilywhites, the Short Grass County, Thoroughbred County or Plainsmen and have four All-Ireland Senior football titles and were the first to lift the old Sam Maguire cup in 1928

'I didn't believe there were so many fans out there.' DJ Carey comments on the reaction to his announced retirement in 1998 and his decision to change his mind.

May 29th

In a first round Munster Senior hurling match on this day in 1949 Jack Lynch scored 1-6 to help Cork to a replay against Tipperary. Tommy Doyle who had the task of marking Christy Ring kept the great player scoreless in both games and Tipperary went on to win the game after extra time 2-8 to 1-9.

Paddy Doherty who won his first All-Ireland Senior football medal in 1950 had played professional soccer with Lincoln Town. On returning to Ireland he had to first sit out his ban under Rule 27 before joining the Down panel.

'In all the years that I had been hurling for Wexford the man above wasn't on our side. He wasn't even giving us a fair chance, he didn't even give us a fifty-fifty.' Martin Storey on bad luck for Wexford before making the break through in the All-Ireland Final of 1996.

May 30th

'I pulled back the midfield and forwards to defend our lead, it is always dangerous to try and defend a lead in Gaelic games. It is better to keep your shape, particularly in the midfield and half-forward areas.' Brian McEniff the Donegal football manager on the danger of trying to hold onto a lead, the approach cost them a league game against Dublin in 1992. McEniff learned the lesson and applied it to good effect to win the All-Ireland final against Dublin later in the year.

Kilkenny are known as the Cats, Noresiders or Marble County and have thirty-one All-Ireland Senior titles in hurling. Between 1904 and 1913 they appeared in seven finals winning them all.

'It's all part of the setup for an All-Ireland final. You have to be able to take it. Some players don't like talking and that's understandable but the media has a job to do and we've a job to do and both of us have to get on with it.' Pá Laide of Kerry discusses media pressure.

May 31st

Kerry play at Fitzgerald Stadium, Killarney and Austin Stack Park, Tralee with a capacity of 50,000 and 12,000 each. FitzGerald stadium is certainly one of the most scenic venues in Ireland and was officially opened on this day in 1936 and is named in honour of the great Kerry footballer Dick 'Dickeen' FitzGerald who wrote the famous guide 'How to Play Football' in 1914.

Footballer Kevin Moran won two All-Ireland Senior football medals with Dublin in 1976 and 1977 before going on to have a successful career with Manchester United.

'The Examiner did an opinion poll in Cork there the other day, and 80 per cent of people thought that Roy was wrong. I'm only joking. Eighty per cent thought that Roy was right, and the other 20 per cent were Kerry people up shopping for the day.' Pat Spillane hosting Sportscall on Radio One in June 2002 has a little joke about the ongoing saga in Saipan.

June 1st

‘We are probably being written off by everyone other than ourselves, but believe me this team of ours at full-strength still has a lot to give and will go on and give it.’ Justin McCarthy the Waterford manager after defeat to Clare in the Senior hurling championship on this day in 2008. Four days later he resigned as ‘I feel I no longer have the full support of all the players on the team.’ Davy Fitzgerald the Clare hurler takes over and leads the Deise to the All-Ireland final.

Tipperary knocked reigning four-in-a-row All-Ireland Senior hurling champions Cork out of the championship on this day in 1945. The teams met in the Munster semi-final at Thurles with the Premier county winning 2-13 to 3-2, Tipperary had scored 1-9 in the second half to Cork’s 1-1 having drawn the first half.

The new Hogan stand is officially opened on this day in 1959.

June 2nd

Kilkenny are delared the 1911 All-Ireland Senior hurling champions on this day in 1912 by virtue of a walkover. Limerick the other finalists had refused to play a rescheduled game in Thurles after the first match in Cork had been ruled unplayable due to poor weather. Despite protests from Limerick and Central Council giving them another opportunity to play at Thurles the matter could not be resolved and the title was awarded to Kilkenny. The Cats later played an improvised final against the beaten Tipperary finalists, possibly the first 'back door' game? Kilkenny went on to win their first ever three in a row, a feat not matched until 2008.

'A lunatic from Clare talking rubbish at the moment ... I know Ger very well and it's sad to see him descend to that level. Inferiority is what I believe it is, a serious sense of inferiority to descend to that silly talk.' Brian Cody responds to Ger Loughnane's pre-All-Ireland allegation in 2007 that Kilkenny were a cynical team.

June 3rd

'In my days as a referee I always tried to be on the side of the field away from the side on which the ball was. In that way I got a side on view of the play. I never believed that the referee should always be up and down the middle of the pitch.' Peter McDermott on refereeing. In his playing days he won an All-Ireland medal with Meath when they beat Cavan in the 1949 final and played on the Meath team beaten by Mayo in 1951. He was inducted into the Hall of Fame at the All Star awards in 1989.

When Roscommon captained by Tom Heneghan won their first ever National League football title in 1979, at the expense of Cork 0-15 to 1-3, it was against a side that had missed a penalty and kicked a total of thirteen wides.

'It's a terrible game from every point of view when you lose it, it's as simple as that.' John O' Mahony former Galway football manager on losing.

June 4th

'A few weeks ago there was a grand match of hurling at Crumlin Commons between the Provinces of Leinster and Munster, in which the former came off victorious. In consequence of this, last Tuesday a chosen set from Munster engaged an equal number of their conquerors at the same exercise and made their utmost efforts to retrieve their honour, but all to no purpose: for Leinster after about an hour's struggle gained a complete victory.' A report in Faulkner's Dublin Journal on this day in 1748 describes a game of hurling between Leinster and Munster.

In 1998 Offaly become the first county to win the All-Ireland hurling final having lost the provincial title under the new rules introduced in 1997. They beat Kilkenny in the All-Ireland final by six points having lost to them in the Leinster final by five points.

June 5th

'You could write the Meath tactics on the back of a postage stamp - just kick it up there. Some people would say it's bogman football.' Colm O'Rourke expresses concern with the Meath approach on RTÉ in 2007.

'But you are bogmen.' Joe Brolly provides some balance to the debate.

'The psychology of life is what I talk about. Each day brings a new story, and a new opportunity to develop, to grow. Players have to do that physically, and mentally, and sure psychology comes into that. But you also have to use the experiences you've had before to be of benefit to you in whatever circumstance you find yourself in during a game.' Mickey Harte the Tyrone manager on the importance of using psychology with his players.

June 6th

Cork play at Páirc Uí Chaoimh, with a capacity of 48,500. The county has 129 clubs. The county ground was originally known as the Athletic Grounds but after major redevelopment it was renamed on this day in 1976 in honour of Pádraig Ó Caoímh the former general secretary of the GAA.

The soldiers of the 79th Irish Battalion at Camp Shamrock in the Lebannon watched the All-Ireland Senior football final live for the first time in 1996 when Mayo met Meath in a drawn match.

'Tyrone have a lot of bad players. Brian Dooher is a bad player. I have a very expensive hat and I will eat it on this show if Tyrone win an All-Ireland and Brian Dooher is on the team.' Colm O'Rourke 2003. Tyrone won the All-Ireland in 2003 with Brian Dooher following with two more in 2005 and 2008.

June 7th

'Two bad teams out there.' Mick O'Dwyer calls it as he sees it in a comment to the Dublin manager, Tom Carr, after his Kildare charges get a draw in the Leinster championship on this day in 1998.

'There can be no one who isn't acutely aware of the scourge of unemployment and enforced emigration. Many GAA clubs have been devastated by the numbers who have left to find employment elsewhere.' 1993 report to Congress.

'What pisses me off most of all is players, young fellas, telling you how to play the game and all the sacrifices they made. Telling you that there should be government grants at the end of it and how they felt their image rights were being infringed upon. You're playing for your county. There are kids out there who'd love to do it.' Former Kerry footballer Dara Ó Cinnéide.

June 8th

'We did what Cormac would have wanted us to do. It was never going to be an easy day but we feel we are positive people and positive footballers.' Mickey Harte Tyrone manager speaking in 2003 on Tyrone's 2-11 to 1-5 defeat of Mayo in their first match after the death of their captain Cormac McAnallen.

The Kerry Ladies' football team won nine All-Ireland finals in a row between 1982 and 1990.

'He questioned our commitment, he said we didn't hurl with commitment or passion. At stages he got booed - but that was mostly on the ticket issue. He takes the decision to make a big speech at the losers' function because everyone wants to go to the winners'. But the reason should be to pick them up, not to tell them they were useless.' Limerick's trainer Dave Mahedy on GAA president Jack Boothman's speech at the losers' dinner in 1996.

June 9th

Mick O'Dwyer was born on this day in 1936, in Waterville, Kerry. As a footballer he won four All-Ireland Senior football titles, with the Kingdom, and was manager when they won eight more. As manager of Kildare he brought two Leinster titles to the county and a place in the 1998 final, his next charges Laois won Leinster in 2003 from where he moved to the Garden County, Wicklow.

'I hope Wexford still have a nice summer with all their (1798) celebrations, but this Offaly side worked as hard as anyone to get this victory.' Babs Keating after his Offaly side beat Wexford in June 1998. Offaly went on to beat Kilkenny in the All-Ireland Senior hurling final minus Babs Keating.

'No one should ask a player twenty-four hours after losing an All-Ireland if they're going to play on or not. Everybody wants to crawl into a corner right now.' Pat O'Shea the Kerry manager speaking the day after Kerry lost the 2008 All-Ireland Senior football final to Tyrone.

June 10th

'There comes a stage when the appetite is no longer there.' Colm Bonnar who at thirty-four had won a Minor All-Ireland in 1982, an Under-21 in 1985 and Senior All-Irelands in 1989 and 1991 announced his retirement on this day in 1998 from inter-county hurling. In 1991 he also captained the Cashel team, which won county and Munster club honours. His brothers Cormac and Conal were also on the Tipperary winning teams of 1989 and 1991.

Laois are known as the O'Moore County and won their first and only All-Ireland Senior hurling final in 1915 against Cork but have yet to add another Senior title in either code. The final score in the game was 6-2 to 4-1.

In 1997 more than 483,000 people attended All-Ireland hurling championship matches compared with 395,000 in 1996, an increase of 25%.

June 11th

On this day in 1922 Dan Breen, one of the men who fired the first shots in the War of Independence, threw in the ball of the delayed 1920 All-Ireland Senior football final between Dublin and Tipperary. The final had been delayed by the fighting and coincidentally featured the two teams that had been present in 1920 when Crown forces opened fire at a challenge game between the sides. Tipperary who had lost their captain on Bloody Sunday won, 1-6 to 1-2, with Tom Power scoring their goal. It was the Premier county's first All-Ireland in twenty years and would be their last time to win the football final to date.

'He's impossible to dislike. Essentially, he's a man's man. Coleman's style was to buoy everyone up. He'd often say: "you are without doubt the greatest Gaelic footballers I have seen." Joe Brolly on Eamonn Coleman who managed Derry when they won their first All-Ireland Senior football final in 1993. Eamonn Coleman passed away, aged 59, on this day in 2007.

June 12th

'We had the extra man and people will say, "you f**kin' eejits, why didn't you make use of him?" We were dragged all over the place... My first reaction was "good, we have an extra man" but we would have preferred fifteen-a-side. After the sending off, our plan went out the window.' Limerick's trainer Dave Mahedy explains why an extra man is not always good.

'But of course we all know how fickle it can be in football, and you can find yourself on the other side of the fence very quickly.' Pat O' Shea reflects on winning the All-Ireland Senior football final in 2007.

Wexford won their first All-Ireland Senior football title in 1894, as was common at the time they were playing for the delayed 1893 Championship. Wexford were represented by the Young Irelands while the defeated finalists Cork were represented by Dromtariffe, the score was 1-1 to 0-1.

June 13th

Graham Geraghty the Meath footballer also had a two week trial with Arsenal .

'Whoever says the National League is dead must be living in cloud cuckoo land.' Brian Canavan the former Armagh football manager.

'It's disheartening that a lack of discipline is an issue - almost on an annual basis - despite repeated warnings, suggestions and campaigns.' Liam Mulvihill former GAA Director-General speaking in 2004.

'They got the planning permission for a structure of that scale simply because of who they are. The attitude of the Croke Park administrators towards the local people has been beyond contempt. Really, they have refused to recognise the existence of the locals.' Tony Gregory TD.

June 14th

At a hurling match on this day in 1885 Maurice Davin suggested that knocking a ball over the crossbar should be counted as the winner as neither team had scored. By November 1885 the point became an integral part of the rules with separate posts being erected on either side of the goals.

Cork win the home final of the delayed 1901 All-Ireland Senior hurling championship on this day in 1903 when they beat Wexford 2-8 to 0-6. They went on to play, what to many was expected to be a mere formality, the final proper against London several weeks later but were beaten in a shock result to give London their only All-Ireland Senior title.

'Disturbing allegations continue to come from various quarters regarding allegations of breaches of amateur status. The most regular 'noises' are being made with regard to coaches/trainers.' 1994 report to Congress.

June 15th

‘Clearly what happened was wrong and I was out of order to do what I did. I regret what I did.’ Paul Galvin of Kerry who slapped the notebook out of the hand of referee Paddy Russell after receiving a second yellow card, in a Championship game against Clare, on this day in 2008. Galvin was given a six-month ban that resulted in a summer of appeals and counter appeals and saw the player banned from training with the county panel. Galvin returned in dramatic fashion as a sub in the All-Ireland final to participate in the Kingdom’s loss to Tyrone.

Louth Senior football titles: 1910, 1912, and 1957.

‘People have said to me already you did Bill Clinton and Monica Lewinsky a favour. You took them off the front page.’ Jimmy Cooney on ending the All-Ireland Senior hurling semi-final replay between Clare and Offaly four minutes early in 1998.

June 16th

Kildare, represented by Roseberry, win their first All-Ireland Senior football final on this day in 1907 when they played Kerry for the 1905 championship at Thurles winning by a score of 1-7 to 0-5. John Connolly scored the only goal of the game when he bundled in his rebounded shot off the crossbar.

Des Cahill the RTÉ presenter was formerly the chairman of south Dublin GAA Club Cuala that is based outside Dalkey. The club was founded in the 1960s through an amalgamation of the Dun Laoghaire Cuala Casements and Dalkey Mitchells.

'Since she has no control over all thc national territory, Ireland's claim to nationhood is impaired. It would be still more impaired if she were to lose her language, if she failed to provide a decent livelihood for her people at home, or if she were to forsake her own games and customs in favour of the games and customs of another nation.' GAA Official Guidc.

June 17th

Dublin win their first All-Ireland Senior football final in thirteen years on this day in 1923, playing for the delayed 1921 championship. Mayo, represented by Ballina Stephenite's, scored a single point in each half to lose 1-9 to 0-2. It was only Mayo's second appearance in the final and Dublin, represented by St. Mary's were clearly the stronger side though their goal was only scored at the very end.

2003 was the first time two teams from the same province lined up in the All-Ireland football final when Tyrone beat Armagh 0-12 to 0-9.

'Some of the matches I see now the defender is not supposed to be there at all. That honest defending is disallowed, because there's a fella sitting in the stand scrutinising every move the referee makes, and I feel massively sorry for referees. They've been torn apart and slaughtered . . . so that assessor, I would shoot him.' Kilkenny manager Brian Cody on the challenges facing referees and proposed solutions.

June 18th

'You can't be as attached to all the facets of Dublin life as I was and not miss it all sometimes. There are a lot of attachments. Sometimes we might wish that we could be twenty-seven forever, that things would never move on. Not many things are constant.' Brian Mullins of Dublin on retirement from playing.

In June 1887 Gladstone, the British Prime Minister, was presented with an inscribed shield, a hurley and a match ball by the Cork County board in recognition of his work for Home Rule. The presentation was the subject of much lampooning in the Tory press of the time.

'It lasted twenty-five or twenty-seven seconds, but the referee restored order and there was more written about it than there was about Zaire.' Seán Boylan the Meath Manager on the bust up in the 1996 All-Ireland Senior football final replay with Mayo. Meath won 2-9 to 1-11.

June 19th

'There are, one, referee, two linesmen and four, umpires. They will do their jobs. When a ball comes in, it can go to the net, over the bar, be saved, be dropped, come back off the woodwork. Anything can happen. The officials will do their job without anybody watching them. Our job is just to follow the ball.' Sean O'Neill who scored a goal to help Down beat Offaly in the 1961 All-Ireland Senior football final explains what is expected of players. Down Senior football titles: 1960, 1961, 1968, 1991, 1994.

Clare play at Cusack Park, Ennis with a capacity of 28,000. The county has fifty-six clubs.

'I had not just to be careful of the opposition ... I had to watch my back.' Tony Considine the former Clare Senior Hurling manager on the perils of management.

June 20th

'The English game of cricket is very much in vogue in Ireland. It has completely displaced the old athletic exercise of hurling so prevalent some years ago.' Reported in the Nenagh Guardian on this day in 1873

Cavan, the All-Ireland champions, had to make a late rally to earn a draw against Cork in the National League final on this day in the 1948. Cavan went on to win the replay and their first National League title.

Leitrim are known as O'Rourke county, Ridge county, Wild Rose county or simply as lovely Leitrim but have failed to win an All-Ireland in Senior football or hurling. In 1995 they won their first Connacht Senior football championship since 1927.

June 21st

'The best team on that Croke Park pitch today were in white jerseys.' Tommy Carr the Dublin manager addresses the winning dressing room after his team were beaten in a Leinster Championship replay in 1998 that saw forty-nine frees and a sending off from each team. It was the first time Kildare had beaten Dublin in the championship since 1972; they would go on to win their first Leinster title since 1956.

Kilkenny won their third All-Ireland Senior hurling title on this day in 1908 when they beat Cork in the final of the delayed 1907 championship. Jim Kelly scored three goals for the Cats to help them to a, 3-12 to 4-8, one point victory. Kilkenny were represented by Mooncoin and Cork by Dungourney.

'Little things matter. Like, if every hurler had a proper grip by the age four, it would be a huge advantage.' Donal O' Grady former Cork hurling manager on the importance of instilling the basics.

June 22nd

‘Indeed if we continue travelling for the next score years in the same direction that we have been going in for some time past, condemning the sports that were practised by our forefathers, effacing our national features as though we were ashamed of them, and putting on, with England’s stuffs and broadcloths, her masher habits and such other effeminate follies as she may recommend, we had better at once, and publicly, abjure our nationality, clap hands for joy at sight of the Union Jack, and place ‘England’s bloody red’ exultantly above the green.’ Excerpt from Archbishop Croke’s letter agreeing to be patron of the GAA in 1884. The Archbishop died on this day in 1902.

‘The association has no apologies to make to anyone for its policy and rules protecting Irish jobs and Irish industry. We are quite happy that our policy and rules will stand up to any scrutiny in this matter. The rule has been in the rule book for more than 100 years.’ A GAA spokesman responds on this day in 1998 to a report that the GAA might be in contravention of European law in relation to the use of sportswear and equipment.

June 23rd

Cavan club side Ballinagh were suspended for six months on this day in 2008 by the county's Competition Control Committee when a referee was struck after a league game against Killygarry. Three players and four supporters were suspended arising out of the incident where the referee was verbally and then physically abused. The individual who struck the referee was banned for 96 weeks.

'There is a lot of shit going around the county last week, but why should I resign?' Babs Keating former Tipperary boss on the pressure from within, on this day in 2007.

'There won't be a cow milked in Clare tonight.' Marty Morrissey's comment after Clare beat Kerry in the 1992 Munster Senior football final 2-10 to 0-12.

June 24th

Cork appeared in and won their third All-Ireland Senior hurling final on this day in 1894, playing for the delayed 1893 Championship. Represented by Blackrock they beat Confederation from Kilkenny comprehensively 6-8 to 0-2. As was now popular while most of the team was made up of the county champions more and more players were selected from other clubs to put out the best side possible, Blackrock would select teams for Cork until 1932. The location for the final had to be switched to the Phoenix Park at the last moment, as the grass had not been cut at the original venue.

Damian Martin picked up Offaly's first ever All Star award in hurling in 1971.

Kilkenny win their first All-Ireland Senior hurling title on this day in 1906 when they played the delayed final of the 1904 Championship. In a hard fought game they eventually over came Cork to win the game, 1-9 to 1-6, in Carrick-on Suir.

June 25th

‘Strangely enough it was the All-Ireland Colleges final at Croke Park in Dublin, when Neil, who had been in bed with flu for the preceding four days, gave the best display of skill and determination I have ever witnessed on any football field, gaining a winner’s medal and The Man of the Match award in an event that players only get one chance to play in, ever.’ Gerald Lennon when asked in 1998 what was his proudest moment in his son Neil Lennon’s playing career. Lennon who played for Armagh in the 1987 Ulster Minor football final before going on to a successful career with Leicester City and Glasgow Celtic was born on this day in 1971.

Kildare play at St. Conleth’s Park, Newbridge with a capacity of 15,000. The county has fifty clubs.

‘Games grow out of the soil, just as the plants do. Hurling grew out of the soil of Ireland.’ Michael Cusack 1887.

June 26th

On this day in 1892 Cork won the 1890 All-Ireland Senior football final by beating Wexford 2-4 to 0-1. Cork were represented by Midleton, in winning their first Senior football title, while Wexford were represented by the Blues and Whites club. Wexford Senior football titles: 1893, 1915, 1916, 1917, 1918.

'On St. Swithen's Day, about 3 in the afternoon, will be a Hurling Match over the Curragh, between 30 men from each side of the Liffey, for 30 shillings. A barrel of ale, tobacco, and pipes will be given to the hurlers.' Notice in the Dublin Flying Post on this day in 1708.

Maurice Davin the first President of the GAA also set a world record for the throwing of the hammer at a meet in Lansdowne Road in 1876.

June 27th

Tipperary won the 1908 All-Ireland Senior hurling title when they beat Dublin in a replay on this day in 1909 at Athy. Tony Carew scored two goals in the second half to secure the win for the Premier county, 3-15 to 1-5. Kilkenny who were now becoming a feature of Championship finals had withdrawn from the 1908 campaign in a dispute over the Railway Cup.

The Kildare team that played Kerry in the first of three games for the famous 1903 home championship final, on this day in 1905, dyed their boots white to match their all white colours, Kerry wore red.

'We wanted to go somewhere they don't know anything about hurling, and it was either Thailand or Tipperary.' Ger Loughnane.

June 28th

'We were completely shapeless in the last quarter of the game, having played so successfully for fifty-five minutes following a particular game plan, we began to panic. We started to defend our lead. The midfielders and half-forwards played too deep.' John Maughan explains what went wrong in the 1996 All-Ireland Senior final when Mayo appeared to have put Meath away but allowed them back into the game for a draw. Mayo Senior football titles: 1936, 1950, and 1951.

The first Poc Fada competition is held in 1961.

'There is no middle ground with us; we are brilliant or we are useless. In Cork, when they lose, next year or the next game is on the way. Even after the strike, people said sure it's no harm to get a break; a negative turned into a positive. Any adversity makes them stronger. They develop on that. They thrive.' John Meyler Wexford manager and former Cork hurler compares Wexford to Cork.

June 29th

Maurice Davin, the first President and founding member of the GAA, is born on this day in 1842. A well-known athlete of the time he set the world record for hammer throwing in 1876 when he threw one hundred and thirty one feet and six inches.

'We cannot afford to allow the bedrock of the game to be undermined. This will happen if the chronic shortage of games is not addressed as a matter of urgency.' GAA director general Liam Mulvihill on the problems caused by foot-and-mouth disease in 2001.

'Rumours will always circulate. Some people have their own agendas but you have got to be above all that.' Former Tipperary hurling boss Ken Hogan.

June 30th

In the replayed and much delayed 1905 All-Ireland Senior hurling final Kilkenny wore the famous black and amber colours for the first time in a final on this day in 1907. Kilkenny won the game against Cork 7-7 to 2-9 with Jim Kelly scoring 5-2 for the Cats. Kilkenny were represented by Erin's Own and Cork by St Finbarr's. Kilkenny play at Nowlan Park, with a capacity of 30,000.

Pat Critchley picked up Laois' first ever All Star in hurling in 1985.

'I went straight to my parents. I knew where they were in the stand and my wife and her family. A very emotional moment, something I'll remember for the rest of my life.' Peter Queally the Waterford hurler on winning the Munster final on this day in 2002, Waterford's first in thirty-nine years, reminds everyone what the motivation is. Waterford Senior hurling titles 1948, 1959.

July 1st

Kerry won their second All-Ireland Senior football final on this day in 1906, playing in the much delayed 1904 final, beating Dublin 0-5 to 0-2. In a very close final, played in Cork, the Kingdom only managed one score in the second half but Dublin failed to register any. Dick 'Dickeen' Fitzgerald was the scorer of Kerry's second half point while the team was captained by Austin Stack.

Limerick are known as the Shannonsiders or the Treaty county and have seven Senior hurling titles and two Senior football titles to their credit.

'We have seen numerous instances of club programmes being cancelled at short notice because the inter-county team manager wanted to have full control over his 30 players for a particular period. The attitude which allows the demands of thirty people to over-rule the requirements of thousands of other people is one which needs to be changed.' Former GAA Director-General, Liam Mulvihill.

July 2nd

'I think it would probably be better if you played the Leinster final in Nowlan Park and packed in 28,000 people and had a great atmosphere. Forget about Croke Park. Bring that full-house intensity rather than have people rattling around Croke Park.' John Meyler Wexford hurling manager 2002.

Sean Óg Sheehy followed his father's footsteps when he captained Kerry to the 1962 All-Ireland Football title. His father John Joe led Kerry to victory in 1926 and 1930.

'There's a black and amber umbrella casting a shadow over the Leinster Championship. What do you do with an umbrella but take it down. At the minute we're not good enough to.' John McIntyre Offaly hurling manager on being beaten 1-27 to 1-13 by Kilkenny.

July 3rd

Cork meet Dublin in the home final of the 1902 All-Ireland Senior hurling championship on this day in 1904. Cork beaten in the previous years final by London are taken to a replay 1-7 to 1-7. They beat Dublin in the replay to get a chance of revenge and do so in the final when they hold London to no score at the official opening of the Athletic Grounds in Cork.

Mayo win their fifth National league football title in a row when they beat Wexford in the final on this day in 1938 at MacHale Park, 3-9 to 1-3.

'Everyone deserves a trial. Even Saddam Hussein got a trial. One question I have is what was I sacked for? A former manager commented on some of these people, referring to mushrooms. But he was being very unfair to mushrooms. They grow on their own and they can stand on their own. The people involved here can't.' Tony Considine on the Clare County Board after he was sacked as hurling manager.

July 4th

A porposal is put to a GAA meeting on this day in 1885 that crossing the end line five times would result in the scoring of a point. At this stage points were not formally recognised as scores and would not be until later that year, a goal was still to outscore any number of points until 1892.

Dick 'Dickeen' Fitzgerald the Kerry footballer who wrote the first instructional manual for the game 'How to Play Gaelic Football' in 1914 was a member of the first All-Ireland winning Kerry football team in 1903.

'They did so for the future of the association, for its members and for its players alone. They did not contemplate or envisage that the dream could become the envy of many, the raison d'etre or the outpouring of bile from a lobby who could not conceal the ideological anathema to the GAA, a lobby that regularly supplemented revisionism with amnesia.' Liam Mulvihill on building Croke Park and the criticism the GAA received on Rule 42.

July 5th

In 1998 Derry got through to their first Ulster hurling final since 1931 when they beat the reigning champions Down in the semi-final. Despite leading 1-6 to 0-8 at half time Antrim were simply too strong in the second half, scoring eight times without reply at one stage, and won their thirty ninth Ulster title by three points on this day in 1998.

In a repeat of the previous year's All-Ireland Senior football final Dublin and Cork meet to decide the delayed 1907 championship, on this day in 1908. Dublin win their second All-Ireland final in a row by a score of 0-6 to 0-2.

'The difference between winning a club and a county All-Ireland is when you get a slap on the back after the club match, you actually know the person when you turn around.' Thomas Meehan of Caltra on winning the 2004 football club final.

July 6th

Central Council agrees on this day in 1888 to go ahead with the proposed visit of GAA hurlers and athletes to the United States to promote the Association and Gaelic sports in general. The cost was estimated at £1,000, which was raised through subscriptions and donations. The trip became known as the US 'Invasion' and poor planning, resulting in lower attendances than expected, left the GAA in a poor financial position until the turn of the century. In addition many athletes remained in the states depriving the sport of top performers in the early years.

In the Munster final played on this day in 1993 Tipperary were champions for the thirty-fifth time after they beat Clare 3-27 to 2-12. Having led the game 2-11 to 0-3 after twenty-four minutes the Premier county were simply uncatchable. It was the second time for Tipperary to beat the Banner county by double scores having done so in their previous Munster final meeting in 1967.

July 7th

‘There has been a negative attitude among some of the players who seemed to have preferred rugby to hurling when it suited them but criticism of me in some newspapers, inspired by players, left me with no alternative to step down.’ Babs Keating comments on his resignation as Offaly manager on this day in 1998.

‘I didn’t mind a fella who wanted to know why or to argue the toss. That was good. He had to understand, though. In the end we would do it my way.’ Kevin Heffernan former Dublin Manager.

‘I remember Anthony Daly saying that he was never sure whether to eat a bowl of soup or a full meal for his lunch because he wasn’t sure what the evening’s session was going to be like.’ Michael McNamara, Clare’s hurling trainer in 1995 when they won their first All-Ireland since 1914 on the importance of varying training from anything from five mile runs to something short and snappy.

July 8th

'The Northern boys made Kerry revise their thinking. Kerry teams now do a lot of ball work in tight and confined spaces.' Jack O'Connor former Kerry football manager.

'There is still a doubt in my head. January came and I felt I should be enthusiastic for it and I wasn't. I hate standing in Crusheen and the wet league Sundays and the ball slow and fellas rolling over one another like drowsy cattle.' Ger Loughnane considers retirement in February 1999.

'The GAA needs Dublin. Dublin needs the GAA. I hope the Leinster Council acknowledge the fact that Kildare and Dublin put 78,000 people into Croke Park today.' Tommy Lyons the Dublin manager in 2002 after the Leinster final win over Kildare.

July 9th

Clare win the Munster Senior hurling final on this day in 1995 by beating Limerick 1-17 to 0-11, a game in which Davy Fitzgerald the Clare goalkeeper scored a penalty for the banner county. They would go on to win the All-Ireland for the first time since 1914.

Crossmaglen Rovers are given back parts of their pitch and club requisitioned by the British Army, almost three decades earlier, on this day in 1999.

'Under pretence of a hurling match.' A letter on this day in 1667 from Lord Orrery describes a meeting to take place in Tipperary.

'As you get older you realize what you're walking into and you get even more nervous.' John Doyle Tipperary hurler on entering Croke Park.

July 10th

'It was the first Kerry-Cork final, and that meant bragging rights for the next 100 years. So it was a game we couldn't lose, really.' Aidan O' Mahony of Kerry on what was at stake when the two sides met in the 2007 All-Ireland final.

Longford are known as the Slashers and their motto is 'Gaisce agus Glaine.' They have a single Junior football All-Ireland title, having failed to win a Senior All-Ireland in either code. They won their only Leinster Senior football title in 1968.

'We've been there, seen the flip side of it, so you have to take the bad with the good and we don't want to begrudge Armagh. Winners takes all in an All-Ireland final and we were just one point short of a draw or two points short of winning it.' Dara Ó Cinnéide the Kerry player on losing to Armagh in the 2002 All-Ireland Senior football final.

July 11th

'Like sheep running around in a heap.' Babs Keating's on his Offaly team after losing the Leinster final in 1998. Keating resigned shortly afterwards and Offaly went on to win the All-Ireland.

Waterford won their first All-Ireland Senior hurling title in 1948 when they beat Dublin in the final 6-7 to 4-2. They won again in 1959 beating Kilkenny and were beaten in the 1963 final by the Cats. They would not reach another final until 2008 when they again faced the might of Kilkenny losing by twenty-eight points.

'He's making it look like the Offaly players are idiots and undisciplined. It's stupid and unfair.' Offaly player Johnny Pilkington responds to manager Bab Keatings criticism of the team after their Leinster final defeat in 1998. Keating resigns in response and Offaly go on to win the All-Ireland.

July 12th

With an eight-point gap at half time Waterford made a magnificent recovery to draw the Munster Senior hurling final on this day in 1998. Helped by an Anthony Kirwan goal just twenty-five seconds into the second half Waterford never gave up with Paul Flynn scoring another goal just two minutes from the end. However Waterford would rue a missed free by Flynn only seconds from the final whistle with Clare making no mistakes in the replay winning 2-16 to 0-10. Both teams however were knocked out in the semi-finals, Waterford had beaten Galway through the back door, leaving two Leinster teams to play the final.

'I'd get rid of the most infuriating rule in the book, the Square Rule. That a forward has to stand there and refrain from playing the ball dropping in, while the keeper swans around like Rudolf Nureyev, is a mockery of the game.' Gerald McCarthy, Cork hurling Manager.

July 13th

Despite making their first apperance in a Leinster final in 1901 and another four appearances over the next seventy-nine years Offaly had to wait unitl this day in 1980 to win their first ever Leinster Senior hurling title beating Kilkenny 3-17 to 5-10. Captained again in the following year by Padraig Horan Offaly woud lift the Leinster title for a second time in 1981 and go on to add a first All-Ireland Senior hurling title to their list of honours in the same year.

In 1997 Tipperary were the first team to reach the All-Ireland Senior hurling final having already lost a provincial final under the new 'back door' system introduced that year. However they lost to the Munster Champions Clare again.

'My father used to have a saying: a big mouth is good for cooling soup.' Pete Finnerty the former Galway hurler responding to Ger Loughnane's suggestion that Kilkenny are a dirty team.

July 14th

'Well, it can't have helped. I don't think it was said in a manner designed to criticise Joachim but it probably appeared so.' Wexford PRO Pat Murphy admits a reported discussion where hurling manager Joachim Kelly was described as the 'last resort' by the county board may have contributed to his resignation on this day in 2000. The resignation followed a heavy defeat to Offaly in the championship.

Meath won their first Leinster Senior football title in 1895 but didn't win another until 1939.

'The kicking of Maurice was what got us through. He was the difference between the two teams. He deserves all the credit he will get from today. Maurice is getting the All-Ireland medal he deserves. He is truly exceptional.' Pá Laide speaking in 1997 on Maurice FitzGerald's role in Kerry winning their first All-Ireland in 11 years.

July 15th

The first ever Leinster Senior hurling final was played at Portlaoise on this day in 1888. Kilkenny, represented by Mooncoin, beat Dublin, represented by Kickhams, 0-7 to 0-3. Unfortunately the All-Ireland final never materialised with the championship unfinished in that year and Kilkenny had to be content with the Leinster title.

While the Cork colours are red jerseys and white shorts they were originally blue and saffron. They wore the famous red for the first time on this day in 1920 when playing in the delayed 1919 All-Ireland Senior hurling final. They won 6-4 to 2-4 against Dublin and decided to stick with the colours, apparently the original strips had been taken by the British army in a raid on the offices of the Cork County Board during the ongoing War of Independence.

Louth known as the Wee County or Boynesiders have three Senior football titles, their first coming in a walkover from Kerry in 1910.

July 16th

The 1944 Munster final and the subsequent replay became known as the bicycle finals. Restrictions during the 'Emergency,' brought about by the Second World War, meant people were only allowed to either walk or cycle to the finals in Thurles. Johnny Quirke of Cork made sure of the draw scoring three out of the six goals scored for the Rebels against Limerick, 6-7 to 4-13, on this day in 1944. In the replay eighteen thousand turned up by foot or on bicycle to see a Christy Ring goal, from forty yards out, decide the match in the last minute of play.

Cork win the home final of the 1904 All-Ireland Senior hurling championship when they beat Kilkenny on this day in 1905, 8-9 to 0-8, at Dungarvan. It is Kilkenny's fifth time to reach the final with nothing to show. Cork go on to beat London for the second year in a row to take the title.

Offaly Senior football titles: 1971, 1972, 1982.

July 17th

A demonstration of the new game Camóguidheacht, the future camogie, took place on this day in 1904 at a feis in Navan. The name was taken from Gaelic word camóg an alternative word for hurley and was thought up by Tadgh Ó Donnchadha.

Dublin only manage to score a single point in the replay of the 1902 home final of the All-Ireland Senior hurling championship on this day in 1904. Cork go on to keep London scoreless in the final.

'We did register some big scores early on in the championship but you need to put the ball over the bar on the day. We didn't do that. It was as simple as that.' Former Mayo manager John Maughan on what it takes to win an All-Ireland.

July 18th

Nicky Rackard of Rathnure was the captain of the Wexford Senior hurlers in 1951 when they won Leinster for the first time since 1918. On this day in 1954 he scored 6-4 against Dublin to give Wexford the Leinster title, 8-5 to 1-4. He had outscored the whole opposition by five goals but despite this and scoring 7-7 in the semi he was still on the losing side in the All-Ireland final against Cork. At thirty-three he won his first All-Ireland when the Slaneysiders beat Galway in the 1955 final. Rackard was to add another All-Ireland medal the next year when they beat Cork and stopped Christy Ring adding a ninth title.

Cork and Tipperary met for their fifth Munster Senior hurling final in a row on this day in 1954. Cork inspired by a goal from a twenty-one yard free by Christy Ring and the making of a second goal from the Glen Rovers and Cork great beat Tipperary and went on to win a third All-Ireland in a row.

July 19th

Clare Senior footballers under the management of Mayo man John Maughan beat Kerry in the Munster final at Limerick 2-10 to 0-12 on this day in 1992. This would be the last game for Jack O'Shea who announced his retirement that evening, having won seven Senior All-Ireland titles.

Laois appearing in a Leinster Senior football final for the first time since their last win in 1889 were beaten by Kildare 2-3 to 0-6 in 1929. On this day seven years later they would have their revenge when they beat the same side, 3-3 to 0-8. While they reached the All-Ireland final they were no match for a very strong Mayo side who beat them 4-11 to 0-5.

Mohammed Ali fought Al Blue Lewis at Croke Park on this day in 1972.

July 20th

Pat Roe the Offaly football manager becomes the fourth football manager of the weekend to step down on this day in 2008. All came at the end of poor results in the qualifiers. Donal Keoghan the Cavan manager quit after defeat to Kildare, Luke Dempsey of Longford after defeat to Laois, Colm Coyle of Meath after a nine point loss to Limerick and Pat Roe's was due to a loss to Down. Liam Kearns of Laois followed less than two weeks later and Paul Caffrey the Dublin boss added his name to the list in August to remind everyone there is pressure at the top.

'I saw some fella in the paper this morning saying it was all about money for me. I would never even dream about money. This is about satisfaction. Today can't be bought. I'm thrilled and delighted.' Mick O' Dwyer in 1998 as Kildare win the Leinster Senior football title for the first time since 1956.

July 21st

Longford play at Pearse Park, Longford with a capacity of 10,000. The county won their only ever Leinster Senior football final on this day in 1968 when they beat Laois 3-9 to 1-4 at Croke Park. They had appeared in one previous final in 1965 when Dublin had proven too strong, they have not appeared in another Leinster final since.

'There is no worry about anything else. It is the pureness of the game. Everyone experiences the pain and everyone experiences the enjoyment when it is over. It is right across the board and there is no other hidden agenda in the room.' Pat O'Shea the Kerry football manager, on what it is all about, in 2008.

'I'm not giving away any secrets like that to Tipp. If I had my way, I wouldn't even tell them the time of the throw-in.' Ger Loughnane.

July 22nd

‘Dinny would be better off talking up his own team really and we’re taking very little notice of what he said down here in Cork.’ Dinny Barry-Murphy the Cork Senior hurling manager responds to criticism of the Cork team by Antrim Manager Dinny Cahill on this day in 2004, Cork went on to win the All-Ireland.

‘Everyone got their money’s worth except the boys in front of me who got in for nothing and got paid for it. Good luck!’ Brian Cody the Kilkenny hurling manager to reporters after his side beat Galway in the championship on this day in 2006.

‘I bet £100,000 to a ha’penny that we won’t get a replay.’ Offaly manager Michael Bond on the 1998 All-Ireland hurling semi-final replay with Clare, when referee Jimmy Cooney blew up early. Offaly got a replay and went on to win the All-Ireland.

July 23rd

Dick 'Dickeen' FitzGerald scored a last minute goal against Kildare in the delayed 1903 home All-Ireland Senior football final on this in 1905. The goal was disputed and a new fixture was made which went to a replay, eventually won by Kerry who then beat London in the final proper. It has been reasonably argued that this goal saved the GAA from financial ruin as the three fixtures, with record crowds for the time, put the GAA finances back on a level footing for the first time since the financially disastrous American 'invasion' trip of 1888. In addition the games captured the public imagination and the popularity of the games grew.

'Old wounds are being let lie. This is my new job, managing Westmeath for the next two years and, whether we're playing Real Madrid or someone else, I'll be trying my best to beat them.' Páidí Ó Sé on taking on the manager's job at Westmeath in 2004 and the possibility of switching codes?

July 24th

Leitrim win the Connacht Senior football title for the first time since 1927 under the management of Mayo man John O'Mahony, beating his home county 0-12 to 2-4, on this day in 1994 at Hyde Park.

Louth win the Leinster Senior football final for the first time in thirty-nine years on this day in 1943. A key player on the team that beat Laois 3-16 to 2-4 was Eddie Boyle playing at full back. He won two Senior county titles with his club Cooley Kickams and another with Dublin club Seán McDermott's in 1947. He never got to win an All-Ireland Senior medal as Louth would not win another title until 1957.

Wexford turned up for the Leinster Senior hurling final on this day in 1977 minus the team jerseys. In borrowing an unnumbered set they created a few problems for the RTÉ commentator of the day Mick Dunne. Numberless Wexford went on to win their second title in a row 3-17 to 3-14.

July 25th

Tommy 'The Boy Wonder' Murphy of Graiguecullen wins his first Leinster Senior football title with Laois on this day in 1937 when they beat Louth 0-12 to 0-4. Despite being only sixteen he went on to score a goal against Kerry in a replayed semi-final of that year when Laois lost by a point. He played in another two All-Ireland semi-finals but Laois just failed to make the breakthrough. In the 1946 Leinster final he kicked eight points against Kildare for a 0-11 to 1-6 win. He was picked in midfield for the Football Team of the Millennium in 1999.

Tyrone play at Healy Park, Omagh with a capacity of 53,000.

'The best feeling I have ever had.' Waterford fullback Sean Cullinane on what it felt like to beat Tipperary in the Munster Championship.

July 26th

‘To offer our keenest rivals our prime marketing asset, and financial assistance is ludicrous in the extreme. If such a decision is taken it will prove to be the most disastrous decision ever taken in our history.’ Jack Boothman former GAA president on opening Croke Park to other sports.

In 1997 Cavan, under the management of Donegal man Martin McHugh, won the Ulster Senior title for the first time since 1969 beating Derry in the final.

‘In 2002 we had good ones against Tipp and against Clare and ‘06 against Cork was a great team performance. But for us to score 3-30, 3-24 from play? We didn’t dream of it. We got some great scores and great goals. You go to kids matches and see great scores taken and see that freedom in play. It was great to get a bit of that and to score some great goals on All-Ireland final day.’ Henry Shefflin on the nature of Kilkenny’s win in the 2008 hurling final.

July 27th

‘I never enjoyed it in fact. You were meant to be critical of players and I just had too much respect for them. I mean they all have families, they all have to go to work on a Monday morning and, as a person, who played myself, I didn’t feel it was my place to be criticising them.’ Jimmy Barry-Murphy on why he never really enjoyed television punditry.

Louth play at O’Raghallaigh Park, Drogheda with a capacity of 6,000.

‘There weren’t many breaks going our way but when we got level we could see this movement breaking down the field and it had goal written all over it.’ Seán Boylan showing that he can read the game very well in advance of Brian Murphy’s goal for Kildare in the 1998 Leinster final.

July 28th

Kilkenny were ordered to play the beaten Munster finalists, Tipperary, for the delayed 1911 All-Ireland Senior hurling championship on this day in 1912. Originally the final had been awarded to the Cats by virtue of a walkover against Limerick but in an attempt to recover some of the financial loss Central Council arranged this alternative final. The Cats won the game 3-3 to 2-1 in Dungarvan setting them up for the first of three All-Ireland titles in a row.

Limerick Senior football titles: 1887 and 1896.

'As you know, these older guys never lose their class. The sad thing is that it's taken three years to get to Croke Park to remind them what great hurlers they are.' Cyril Lyons the Clare hurling manager on his team's one point victory over Galway in the All-Ireland Senior quarter-final on this day in 2002, Clare went on to lose to Kilkenny in the final.

July 29th

Dublin win their sixth Leinster Senior football title in a row with Kevin Heffernan as their manager beating Offaly 1-8 to 0-9 on this day in 1979. Matching the record set by Wexford in 1918 and folllowed by Kildare in 1931. Three out of the six were converted into All-Ireland winning titles with the last coming in 1977 when Jimmy Keaveney scored 2-6 against Armagh winning 5-12 to 3-6. Dublin in the next year came up against a Kerry side on their way to four-in-a-row.

The Mayo Ladies' football team won their first All-Ireland football title in 1999 adding another in 2000.

'Even though I enjoyed playing football you look at Kilkenny and there aren't that many dual players. And, on that score, Kilkenny have got it right.' Donal O'Grady former Cork hurling manager.

July 30th

New York win their first National League football final on this day in 1950 beating Cavan, who had lost their Ulster title to Armagh only a week earlier. Cavan having won the home decider against Meath lost out to the visitors at Croke Park 2-8 to 0-12.

Laois play at O'Moore Park, Portlaoise with a capacity of 28,500.

Carlow appeared in their third ever Leinster Senior football final on this day in 1944 and beat Dublin, the team who had beaten them on their last two appearances in the final in 1941 and 1942. The final score in the final played in Athy was 2-6 to 1-6, giving Carlow their first every Leinster Senior football title. They were beaten by Kerry in the semi-final who in turn lost out to a great Roscommon side in the All-Ireland final. Carlow have not appeared in the Leinster final since.

July 31st

‘The strange thing about it, the pain did not worry me. When you are playing in an All-Ireland final you are simply intent on giving it everything.’ Gary Kirby of Limerick on playing with a broken finger in the 1996 All-Ireland Senior Hurling final.

Mayo are known as the Maritime county, the Heather county or as the Green above the Red and whose motto is ‘Críost Linn’ have three Senior All-Ireland titles in football, their first coming in 1936.

‘People expected me to go to Galway with a magic wand and next thing an All-Ireland would be won.’ Ger Loughnane, former Clare hurling manager, on the expectations when he became the Galway manager.

August 1st

Dublin win their second three-in-a-row in the All-Ireland Senior football championship when they beat London for the delayed 1908 final on this day in 1909. In a convincing home final Dublin had beaten Kerry 0-10 to 0-3 and London, appearing in the last final proper, were no match losing 1-10 to 0-4. The only real incident of note in the final was a sending off in the first half for a Dublin player reducing the winners to sixteen men under the old rules.

'Personally, this is the realisation of a dream. It means everything. You give your life to playing hurling. The ambition for everybody is to win an All-Ireland medal. I've been hurling with Tipp eight years and won nothing except a couple of national leagues. Winning a Munster championship and All-Ireland makes everything worthwhile, all the sacrifices.' Tommy Dunne the captain of the Tipperary Senior hurling team on winning the All-Ireland in 2001.

August 2nd

London win the All-Ireland hurling final on this day in 1903 at Jones' Road. The game was to decide the 1901 championship. They did it by beating the home champions Cork, 1-5 to 1-4. The exiles were represented by London Emmet's, who contained no less than nine players originally from Cork, and it was to be the first and only time the title would be won by a team not representing the thirty-two home counties. Several reasons were put forward for Cork losing but they would not underestimate the London side again and beat them 3-13 to 0-0 in the final the next year.

Dublin win their seventh All-Ireland Senior football final on this day in 1903 when they played the final of the delayed 1901 championship against London. The final score is another big win for the home final champions, 0-14 to 0-2. Cork had proven more difficult in the home final losing 1-2 to 0-4.

August 3rd

'Hurling needs a Dublin All-Ireland; I said that to them in the dressing room last year and I still say it.' Kilkenny hurler DJ Carey to defeated Dublin players but to no avail.

'The motion is not a proposal to rescind a rule but rather a proposition to alter the fundamental structure of the Association and to open the ranks to those who never accepted us for what we are.' Pat Fanning, GAA President 1970 on a motion to remove the Ban.

'I think it's farcical. I think that 99 per cent of the country felt that Davy was the best keeper over the year and no matter what they say, the reason he didn't get an award is over that suspension. They should just have come out and say he wasn't considered because of the suspension but, of course, that would have taken a bit of courage.' Ger Loughnane's reaction to the omission of Davy Fitzgerald from the 1999 All Star hurling team.

August 4th

On this day in 1918 British Soldiers prevented a camogie match taking place at Croke Park. The game went ahead on the street outside.

'I would not let anybody into the car park, not to mention into Croke Park.' Dan Hoare, Munster Council treasurer on allowing rugby and soccer in Croke Park.

'And I'm into rewarding success as well. If you win an All-Ireland you deserve two or three weeks away somewhere. Or whatever the group wants to do. And there should be no questions asked. What I don't like is this touting teams around, selling pictures of them and all that. I call it arse-boxing. That word is not in the dictionary but it's a good enough word to describe it.' Tommy Lyons the Dublin manager speaking about a new code in 2002.

August 5th

'Meath football is honest-to-goodness football, it's from the heart, it's passionate. To succeed you need the two ingredients and you have both in abundance. The very best of luck to you.' Páidí Ó Sé the Kerry football manager to the Meath team after they defeated the Kingdom in the All-Ireland semi-final in 2001.

Although the first camogie organisation was founded in 1904, the first All-Ireland camogie final was only arranged in 1932, after a meeting to lay down the rules of the competition in Dublin's Gresham hotel.

'Dublin should be divided, using the river Liffey as the boundary, into two 'Counties' - Dublin North and Dublin South.' GAA strategic review report in 2002, recommends what some would argue is the reality of Dublin life should become enshrined in the GAA structure.

August 6th

RTÉ broadcast the first live game for television from Croke Park showing the All-Ireland Senior football semi-final between Kerry and Dublin on this day in 1962.

Seamus Clancy picked up Clare's first ever football All Star in 1992, a year in which his team beat Kerry in the Munster final.

Monaghan play at St. Tiernach's Park, Clones with a capacity of 36,000. The county ground was bought for £700 in 1944 and officially opened on this day in the same year.

Nicky Rackard scored 7-7 for Wexford against Galway in the 1954 All-Ireland Hurling semi-final but lost out to Cork in the final.

August 7th

‘We took some flak in certain quarters but that was the idea, to create awareness amongst players and public that players had got up off their arses and done something rather than just talk about it on barstools until two in the morning.’ Dessie Farrell.

Limerick play at the Gaelic Grounds, Limerick with a capacity of 49,500.

Antrim won their first All-Ireland Senior camogie title in 1967.

‘If you believe soccer, rugby, Gaelic football, ladies’ football and camogie and other sports can all be played on the same pitch then you have to be a bit of a nitwit.’ Bertie Ahern

August 8th

'You'll have to wait a long time for my retirement!' Mick O' Dwyer former Kerry, Kildare, Laois and current Wicklow manager.

'I'm just delighted to get another opportunity ... and isn't it great to give the GAA another half a million?' Tommy Dowd of Meath on replays.

'We won this game between February and May on the training fields of Ballymaguigan and Maghera.' Eamonn Coleman Derry football Manager after a win over Donegal in the Ulster final in 1993.

Dublin created an upset when they beat the reigning champions Cork in 1927 in the All-Ireland Senior hurling final, 4-8 to 1-3. The Dublin side contained nine gardaí, a common feature of Dublin teams at that time.

August 9th

Kildare match Wexford's record of six Leinster Senior titles in a row when they beat Westmeath, 2-9 to 1-6, on this day in 1931. However Kildare could only reap two final wins from their success compared to Wexford's four-in-a-row.

Meath who are known as the Royal county have seven Senior titles in football winning their first All-Ireland in 1949.

'It was a pressure shot but they all are on a day like today. It was on my stronger side and I had a bit of time. As a team we have probably played better. The big thing was that when the questions were asked we were able to answer them.' Jamesie O' Connor on scoring the winner in the 1997 All-Ireland Senior hurling final.

August 10th

Richard Blake from Meath who became secretary of the GAA in 1895 was responsible in his three years of tenure for the standardisation of the size of the football, the introduction of linesmen to assist referees and the fixing of a goal's value at three points instead of five. He opposed political discussion within the GAA and was largely responsible for removing the ban on the police joining the association and the ban on foreign games. This brought him into conflict with members of the IRB who had him removed for unproven charges of financial incompetence. Rule 21 was passed and the ban reintroduced.

'Since the weekend I realised that the association is changing direction altogether. Suddenly I lost interest in doing the voluntary work if the sport ceases to be for sport's sake.' Donal McAnallen brother of the late Tyrone footballer Cormac McAnallen on the grants issue.

August 11th

'There are a lot of country folk living and working in Dublin, and they are probably going back to where they came from and saying, "ah, Dublin this and that."' Dublin goalkeeper Stephen Cluxton explains why the Dubs get such bad press.

Peter McGinnity picked up Fermanagh's first All Star football award in 1982.

Wicklow play at The County Ground, Aughrim with a capacity of 8,000.

'I wonder what would happen if a Meath player did a full frontal on a goalkeeper? What would happen lads? It was a terrible decision. But I don't want to take anything from Dublin because they played beautiful football and deserved it.' Seán Boylan on defeat to Dublin in 2002.

August 12th

'Notwithstanding that Mr. Sheriff Worthington dispersed a surprising multitude of people gathered on a Sunday for a hurling match in the Phoenix Park, they had the audacity to last Sunday evening to assemble again, and repeat their innocent diversion, so well suited to the Sabbath, and so disgraceful to the authorities of the Park, which could easily suppress them, if properly executed.' Report in the Dublin Evening Post on this day in 1779. Almost a hundred years later the early founders of the GAA would face the same opposition to games on the Sabbath. Implementation of the Lord's Observance Act of 1695 by the authorities had become less common but individuals who strongly opposed games on the Sabbath often attacked supporters and players in the early years.

Roscommon Senior football titles: 1943, 1944.

Caleb Crone won an All-Ireland with Dublin in 1942 and another with Cork in 1945.

August 13th

Wexford man Philip Keating was the first goalkeeper to captain his team to the Leinster football title in 1890 when they beat Dublin by 1-3 to 1-2

A special Congress is held in 1923 at which suspensions for Limerick in the Senior hurling final and Kerry in the Senior football final are lifted. Both had refused to meet their All-Ireland final fixture in protest at the non-release of Republican prisoners held in the Civil War. This Congress and the subsequent games are credited with saving the association and going a long way to heal the rift in the GAA caused by the Civil War.

'We're in the worst county, because we're breeding more reporters at the moment than millionaires. Local and national reporters, and some of them wouldn't know how to make a hurl. Or they'd pick up the wrong end.' Babs Keating, after resigning as Tipperary manager in August 2007.

August 14th

Blackrock in Cork were founded in 1883, prior to the formation of the GAA, and up until 1931 were responsible for selecting the county hurling team. This was withdrawn for the 1932 Championship to be replaced by selectors and caused the great Eudie Coughlan of the Blackrock club to decline the captaincy and retire from inter-county hurling. Several other Blackrock players retired and Cork who had won four out of the last six All-Ireland Senior hurling titles would not win another for ten years. Blackrock won their first All-Ireland club final in 1972, the second year of the competition, when they beat Rathnure of Wexford 5-13 to 6-9.

'It is hard to perceive the incredible disruption these events cause to the lives of locals, with people urinating and vomiting in our gardens, the constant knocking and tapping on doors and peering through the windows of terraced houses.' Croke Park Area Residents Alliance.

August 15th

‘My first impression of the man was that he was a fanatic.’ Paddy O’Donoghue of Kildare on the impression Mick O’Dwyer made on him when he first came to Kildare in 1990.

Sligo play at Markievicz Park with a capacity of 17,000.

‘One thing I will say no matter what the story is, there are probably a few guys out there waiting for this moment to have a go at me. They can have it all. When I came into this job I said if I did everything I knew how to do I would be happy with myself. I did everything I thought was possible. Maybe I will have to look at myself and ask myself questions. I will not blame the boys one bit whatsoever.’ Davy FitzGerald, the Waterford Manager in 2008, on taking over the team and their twenty-three point loss to Kilkenny in the final.

August 16th

'It's been a crazy year for results and who is to say there won't be another crazy result or two before it is over.' Paul Caffrey, the Dublin Manager on this day in 2008, as they suffer their biggest championship defeat in thirty years since the 1978 All-Ireland final against Kerry.

Meath played Offaly in the Leinster Senior football final on this day in 1997, losing the game 3-17 to 1-15. Many felt Meath had played out their best football earlier in the championship when it took the reigning All-Ireland champions three games to get past Kildare.

'It is a great source of pride to me that I could, in my innocence, come up here and manage a team that could take ye on and beat ye.' Brian Cody the Kilkenny manager to the Clare team after his side beat them in the All-Ireland semi-final in 1999.

August 17th

Four-in-a-row Senior football champions Kerry are knocked out it the All-Ireland semi-final on this day in 1933 by Cavan. 17,000 supporters turned up to watch the game in Breffni Park where a last minute goal from Vincie McGovern won the game for Cavan, 1-5 to 0-5. Cavan went on to win their first All-Ireland. Cavan Senior football titles: 1933, 1935, 1947, 1948, 1952.

Mayo play at McHale Park, Castlebar with a capacity of 35,000.

Cork lift the Liam McCarthy Cup for the fouth time in a row in 1944, the first and only team to do so. They beat Dublin, 2-13 to 1-2.

'It's just a matter of getting too old.' Vinnie Murphy of Dublin explains why he retired from inter-county football.

August 18th

'The whole heart of the organisation will be gone if the games go professional. I never want to see that. If you haven't the heart in the association, you have nothing.' D.J. Carey.

Galway withdrew from the 1936 All-Ireland Senior hurling semi-final when the referee refused to send off a Limerick player. Galway felt the sending off was necessary to balance the injury sustained by a Galway player during a bust up and subsequent pitch invasion by spectators. Limerick went on to win the final beating Kilkenny 5-6 to 1-5.

'Absolutely pulverised. We were afraid to walk down the street after it. We got beaten again in '94. F***ing won an All-Ireland in '95. Psychologically, it is up to the fellas themselves.' Davy FitzGerald the former Clare player discussing how Clare came back after being hammered in the 1993 Munster final.

August 19th

Noel Skehan set a record in 1983 when he won his ninth All-Ireland Senior hurling title when Kilkenny beat Cork in front of 58,381 spectators at Croke Park.

Matt O'Connor of Offaly club Walsh Island scored 0-7 in the 1982 All-Ireland Senior football final to help his team beat Kerry 1-15 to 0-17 and add an All-Ireland Senior medal to his three Senior Leinster medals. He was picked as an All Star three times and played alongside his brother Richie who was the captain of the team in the 1982 final.

'He kicks the ball lán san aer, could've been a goal, it could've been a point, it went wide.' Micheál Ó Muircheartaigh.

August 20th

Monaghan known as the Oriel County, the Drumlin county or Farney were the first county to win a provincial Senior title when they beat Cavan in a replay of the 1888 Ulster final but have failed to add a Senior All-Ireland title.

'That's a fundamental in hurling. Hard, honest work, blocking and tackling , will win out at the end of the day.' Davy Fitzgerald former Clare hurler and current Waterford manager.

Dermot Earley picked up too All Star football awards in the seventies for Roscommon. His son Dernot picked up another for Kildare in 1998.

'Ring was a God, but Jack - Jack was one of our own.' Dave O'Brien of Glen Rovers on two former team mates Christy Ring and Jack Lynch, speaking after the passing of the later in 1999.

August 21st

'Bail ó Dhía oraibh go léir a cháirde agus fáilte rómhaibh go Páirc an Chrócaigh.' Micheál Ó Hehir's opening lines, on this day in 1938, when he made his first broadcast from Croke Park. The Cusack Stand was officially opened on the same day.

'None. But I was out threshing until 10 o'clock every night. What training would I need?' Paddy Martin of Kildare on his training for the 1928 All-Ireland.

'I was walking up the town one night last winter and I met this guy I kind of knew. He says to me: "Did I hear you got called into the Mayo panel?" I says: "I did, yeah." And he started laughing at me. He says: "What the f★★k do they want you for?"' Footballer Ronan McGarrity in 2004 on his call up to the Mayo panel.

August 22nd

Armagh won the All-Ireland Senior football semi-final in 2002 when in injury time Ray Cosgrave's free kick for Dublin came back off the post to give them a one point win over the Dubs. Armagh went on to beat Kerry by one point in the final, winning their first ever Senior title.

Leitrim play at Páirc Mac Diarmada, Carrick-on-Shannon with a capacity of 14,000. The county has twenty-four clubs.

'The whole point is we are trying to move towards a civilised society that is tolerant and accepts others. We have reached the stage where we are more than happy for the English anthem to be played in Croke Park. It's a fun song, pretty catchy. Who better to save the queen than God himself?' Joe Brolly on the English rugby team playing in Croke Park.

August 23rd

In the 1910 Leinster Senior football final Dublin failed to score in either half, losing to Louth by three points.

Westmeath play at Cusack Park, Mullingar with a capacity of 11,000.

Teddy McCarthy becomes the first player to win both an All-Ireland Senior title in both hurling and football in the same year when his team beat Mayo, 0-11 to 0-9, in the 1990 football final. He was also on the team that had beaten Galway just over two weeks earlier in the hurling final.

'If anyone thinks the games of the empire have a greater call in them than the games of his country, he is welcome to go to them.' Tom Walsh, Kilkenny GAA chairman 1928.

August 24th

‘It wasn’t nice.’ Davy Fitzgerald the Waterford Manager on being down seventeen points at half time in the 2008 Senior Hurling final against Kilkenny.

Waterford play at Walsh Park, Waterford and Fraher Field, Dungarvan with a capacity of 14,000 and 8,000.

Michael Cleary of Tipperary scored a goal from a mis-hit free in the All-Ireland Senior hurling final of 1991 to help his side to a 1-16 to 0-15 win over Kilkenny. Cleary scored 1-6 in the game to match the sore from DJ Carey of 0-9.

‘We went out and we played from minute one to the last minute. That’s what sport is about, going out and giving everything.’ Brian Cody.

August 25th

'The term of Páidí Ó Sé is up and we will have to put in place a new management team.' County Chairman Seán Walsh on this day in 2003.

'It seems to me that nothing short of All-Ireland success is acceptable in Kilkenny. I had a feeling that before Sunday's match I had lost the confidence of the players and, in that situation, the best thing for me and Kilkenny hurling is that I should step down.' Nicky Brennan Kilkenny Manager announces his resignation on this day in 1997.

'If I had solved that I wouldn't be talking to you! It's easy to say but limiting the supply, further out the field, will limit the space inside.' Conor Hounihan, the manager of the Cork footballers who were beaten by Kerry in a replayed semi-final, on being asked how Tyrone should deal with Donaghy, Walsh and Cooper in the 2008 All-Ireland final.

August 26th

Dublin put a stop to Kilkenny's quest for a third All-Ireland Senior hurling title in a row when they won a replay of the Leinster final on this day in 1934. The final score in Portlaoise was 3-5 to 2-2.

'Cork must be in trouble if they have brought Brian Corcoran back. He's finished - and he'll definitely be finished after Sunday. They've been struggling to get scores all year and they have a dreadful centre forward.' Dinny Allen the Antrim manager in 2004 before Cork beat them 2-26 to 0-10 in the quarter-final.

'After the league semi-final we said "OK, we fix A, B C and D." Then we come along today and they open up X, Y and Z. It's hard to take, hard to look at.' Wexford manager John Meyler on the letters Kilkenny produced to win the 2007 Leinster final by double scores.

August 27th

With some similarity to the 1982 final Kerry were also deprived of a record five-in-a-row All-Ireland Senior football championships in 1933 by a goal scored in the final minutes of a game. Kerry lost their quest for five in a row in the semi-final on this day in 1933 when Vincent McGovern of Cavan scored the goal to give them victory, 1-5 to 0-5. Cavan went on to beat Galway in the final.

'It was Manila, Frazier and Muhammad Ali. They slugged each other. Both teams thought they were going to win right to the end. That's what made it so phenomenal.' Jim Brogan former Dublin player, a sub on the day, describes the semi-final clash when Kerry were beaten by Dublin on this day in 1977.

'Let there be no sounding of trumpets as the rule disappears. Nor should there be talk of defeat. If victory there be, let it be a victory for the Association.' Pat Fanning GAA President on the removal of the Ban in 1971.

August 28th

'I'd like to say switching Brian Whelehan from the backs to the forwards was sheer inspiration. But Brian was suffering from a heavy flu, his legs were dead. It is unbelievable that he could play at such a high level and he such a sick man.' Michael Bond the Offaly Manager on Whelehan's score of 1-6 in Offaly's 1998 All-Ireland hurling final win over Kilkenny.

Tyrone Senior football titles: 2003, 2005 and 2008.

'I was following the ball in when all hell broke loose. It was really scary in there. Haymakers were flying from all angles. Frightening is the word. It was the roughest I have ever seen in football or basketball.' Liam McHale of Mayo describes the scene before he got sent off in the 1996 All-Ireland.

August 29th

The first radio broadcast of a GAA match takes place on this day in 1926 when the new national station broadcasts the All-Ireland Senior hurling semi-final match, between Galway and Kilkenny. The first ever commentator was Paddy Mehigan from Cork. Radio broadcast of the 1929 All-Ireland Senior hurling final was not allowed as the association had concerns the new medium would have a negative impact on spectator support. In truth commentators like Micheál Ó Hehir pushed spectator support to new levels as interest was driven on by the action being brought into homes up and down the country.

'The team was picked on Tuesday night, but we told the players to ignore what appeared in the papers and that we'd tell them the actual team on the Sunday morning.' Ger Loughnane the Clare hurling manager explains he released an incorrect team sheet to the press in 1998 to prevent too much exposure to his younger players.

August 30th

‘If you hear anybody from Clare complaining about anything, they do not represent the Clare hurling team or real hurling followers in Clare. The better team won today and we wish you the very best of luck.’ Ger Loughnane the Clare hurling manager addresses the Offaly dressing room after Clare’s defeat in the ‘replay’ of the 1998 semi-final replay that had been blown up three minutes early, on this day that year.

A record 84,856 spectators turned up to watch an All-Ireland hurling final in 1954 when Cork won three in a row to beat Wexford 1-9 to 1-6 at Croke Park. 1,760 less people turned up to watch the same teams play again in 1956 when Wexford won their second title in a row, 2-14 to 2-8, making it the second biggest crowd ever to watch a Senior hurling final.

‘I don’t want to be recognized.’ Christy Rings reason for putting on a cap before a match.

August 31st

Henry Kenny the father of Enda Kenny, the leader of Fine Gael, won a Senior football All-Ireland with Mayo in 1936 when they beat Laois 4-11 to 0-5. Mayo forward Josie Munnelly scored 2-3 to outscore the whole opposition with fellow Mayo forward Paddy Moclair matching the Laois score with five points.

'People of Galway, we love you.' Joe Connolly the Galway Senior hurling captain on the occasion of the tribesmen winning their first All-Ireland since 1923 in 1980.

In 1886, at the second Annual Convention of the GAA, Maurice Davin, the first President of the organization, was the only non-IRB member of the GAA executive.

Bobby Beggs won an All-Ireland with Galway in 1938 and another with Dublin in 1942.

September 1st

Wexford win their fifth All-Ireland Senior hurling title on this day in 1968. Having trailed Tipperary by ten points at one stage in the game Wexford made a miraculous comeback to win, 5-8 to 3-12. Wexford had won their last title eight years earlier and would not get their hands on the Liam McCarthy Cup again until this day in 1996, when they beat Limerick 1-13 to 0-14, despite having Éamon Scallan sent off.

Having lost the previous year's All-Ireland Senior hurling final to Cork by twenty-seven points Galway were back in the final on this day in 1929 to prove they deserved to be there. Cork however led by a strong group of Blackrock players won the game, 4-9 to 1-3.

Eddie Keher scores a penalty on this day in 1974 to help Kilkenny win the All-Ireland Senior hurling final against Limerick, the team who had beaten them in the previous year's final. The final score was 3-19 to 1-13.

September 2nd

A crowd of 59,814 spectators turn up at Thurles to watch the 1984 All-Ireland Senior hurling final, played on this day, to mark the centenary of the GAA in that year. Cork won the game beating Offaly 3-16 to 1-12. It was fitting that a team that had won four All-Ireland Senior hurling titles in the first ten years in the history of the association were still winning titles a hundred years later. The appearance in the final of a new force in hurling, at the dawn of a new century of the Association, was equally fitting.

Tipperary playing, on this day, in the 1951 All-Ireland Senior hurling final won their third title in a row. It was Tipperary's second time to achieve a three-in-a-row, while they were the first hurling county to get a second three-in-a-row the bar had been raised by Cork's four-in-a-row seven years earlier. Wexford looking for their first win since 1910 were the beaten finalists, 7-7 to 3-9.

September 3rd

Five thousand fans found themselves locked outside the gates of Croke Park when the ground had swollen to a capacity 45,176 to watch the All-Ireland Senior hurling final on this day in 1933. It was the biggest crowd to turn up at Croke Park at that time. The record crowd saw a second half goal from Kilkenny's Johnny Dunne help the Cats to victory over Limerick, 1-7 to 0-6.

Antrim appear in their first All-Ireland Senior hurling final on this day in 1943 when they were beaten 5-16 to 0-4 by Cork. The Cork team were in the middle of an unprecedented four in a row that would be completed the following year. Antrim had created a sensation by beating Kilkenny, 3-3 to 1-6, in the semi-final and Galway previous to that. Antrim would next appear in an All-Ireland final on this day in 1989 when again they lost out, but this time to Tipperary, 4-24 to 3-9. Nicky English of Tipperary, who were winning their first final in twenty-eight years, scored 2-12 to match the score for the whole Antrim team.

September 4th

Cork win their first All-Ireland hurling final in twelve years, they had not reached the final in ten, on this day in 1966. Gerald McCarthy lifted the cup when they beat a hotly fancied Kilkenny side 3-9 to 1-10.

Dublin win their last All-Ireland Senior hurling final to date when they beat Waterford, appearing in their first ever final, on this day in 1938. The final score was 2-5 to 1-6.

Paddy Reynolds the Meath footballer whose father Pat picked up his county's first All Star in 1971 picked up his own playing for the Royals in 1999.

Wexford win their first All-Ireland Senior hurling final in forty-five years when they beat Galway, who had received a bye to the final without playing a game, on this day in 1955, 3-13 to 2-8.

September 5th

Christy Ring became the first player to win eight All-Ireland Senior hurling medals on this day in 1954 when Cork, with Ring captaining a winning All-Ireland team for the third time, beat Wexford 1-9 to 1-6. The game was played in front of a record 84,856 spectators at Croke Park. This was to be his last All-Ireland win, adding eight hurling medals to one won for Cork in the 1946 All-Ireland Senior football final and four National league medals. At club level he won fourteen Senior county medals in hurling and one in football. When Cork won three-in-a-row for the fourth time in 1978 beating Kilkenny, 1-15 to 2-8, in front of 64,155 spectators at Croke Park Christy Ring was a selector for those three campaigns and would sadly pass away a year later.

Waterford win their first ever All-Ireland Senior hurling final on this day in 1948. Willie Galvin and John Keane scored Waterford's two goals in the first half to give them a 2-5 to 0-2 lead at half time, Dublin never recovered losing 6-7 to 4-2.

September 6th

Offaly make their fisrt ever appearance in an All-Ireland Senior hurling final on this day in 1981 and go on to win the title for the first time ever beating Galway 2-12 to 0-15. 71,348 spectators turned up at Croke Park to watch the game, the biggest crowd for an All-Ireland Senior hurling final since the 1963 final, when Kilkenny beat Waterford.

Tipperary won their first All-Ireland Senior hurling title in nine years when they beat Galway, appearing in the final for the third year in a row, on this day in 1925. Paddy Power scored the opener for the Premier county to help them on their way to a comprehensive win, 5-6 to 1-5. The game also saw a scoreboard used at the Railway end for the first time on the same day Tipperary got their hands on the Liam McCarthy Cup for the first time.

Waterford and Kilkenny played out the first draw in an All-Ireland Senior hurling final in twenty five years when they took the game to a replay, 1-17 to 5-5, on this day in 1959.

September 7th

‘In 1934, it couldn’t be done. In 1976, it couldn’t be done. In 1984, it couldn’t be done. In 1994, it couldn’t be done. In 2004. But not in 2008.’ Kilkenny captain James Fitzpatrick on winning three-in-a-row on this day in 2008 when they beat Waterford by twenty-three points in the All-Ireland Senior hurling final. Not since the Cats last completed three-in-a row in 1913 had the county been able to repeat the feat despite numerous opportunities.

Tipperary win the 1930 All-Ireland Senior hurling final on this day, beating Dublin 2-7 to 1-3, in a year that also saw the Premier county win the Junior and Minor All-Ireland hurling titles also.

Galway in front of 64,895 spectators at Croke Park won their second All-Ireland Senior hurling title, after a gap of fifty-seven years, on this day in 1980 when they beat Limerick 2-15 to 3-9.

September 8th

'John Hoyne was warming up in the dressing room and he got a slap of a hurl in the head from someone. He got four staples before he went out. That was just the warm-up.' Henry Shefflin on the Kilkenny warm up before the All-Ireland on this day in 2002, they won 2-20 to 0-19 over Clare. Shefflin scored 1-7 in the game and along with DJ Carey's score of 1-6 they made all but seven points of the Kilkenny score, matching the Clare score between them.

'In those days, there was one microphone which covered the commentator, the crowd, the band, everything. This was a round thing that was up over my head in the box. Lightning was flashing off this and going along the wires. It could have been frightening, but the match was so good you didn't notice it.' Micheál Ó Hehir on covering the 1939 All-Ireland Senior hurling final, the aptly named 'Thunder and Lightening Final,' between Cork and Kilkenny. Kilkenny won 2-7 to 3-3.

September 9th

'I think that in life, if you keep hopping your head off a stone wall, eventually you will get a break.' Nicky English the Tipperary manager after beating Galway 2-18 to 2-15 on this day in 2001 to win the All-Ireland hurling final.

Galway received a bye through to the All-Ireland Senior hurling final on this day in 1928 but paid for their lack of match fitness when Cork stormed to a 6-12 to 1-0 win. A bad injury to Galway player Mick King in the first half, in which he broke his leg, unsettled the tribesmen and Galway didn't register a score in the second half. Mick and Paddy Ahearne scored five of the Cork goals between them.

'It was a dull, humid day, there wasn't a breath of wind in Croke Park. Suffocating. Uneasy feeling.' Páidí Ó Sé the Kerry footballer describes the 1977 semi-final clash when they were beaten by Dublin.

September 10th

Kilkenny's DJ Carey scored 2-4, his first goal coming after six minutes, to help his side beat Offaly in the All-Ireland Senior hurling final on this day in 2000, 5-15 to 1-14.

'I remember living in a terrace and being lucky that there was a wall to puck the ball against on our house. T'was solitary at the time. When there were a few lads around we would go to the field.' Donal O'Grady former Cork hurler and manager.

'Yeah, there were highs and lows, but winning wouldn't be so nice if losing wasn't so terrible. I felt that three years in this seat is enough for any sane man.' Tommy Lyons former Dublin manager comments on his resignation in 2004.

September 11th

'Were it not for the GAA when it stood for Ireland, England in her great war would have annexed much of her finest bone and muscle that was saved for Ireland.' Michael Collins in a speech at the Leinster final on this day in 1921.

Dublin represented by Bray Emmets, who would later play in Wicklow, win the All-Ireland Senior football final on this day in 1904. They were playing in the delayed final of the 1902 championship. Dublin were easy winners notching up 2-6 in the first half to win the game 2-8 to 0-4 against London. Tipperary had been a closer contest in the home final 0-6 to 0-5, London as a province played the winners of the home final at that time.

Cork win their thirthieth All-Ireland Senior hurling final on this day in 2005. Ben O'Connor scored Cork's only goal in a 1-21 to 1-16 victory over Kilkenny. Kilkenny now two titles behnd Cork needed a hat trick of titles to overtake them –which is excatly what Brian Cody's men did in 2008.

September 12th

The first All-Ireland Senior hurling final not to produce a goal is played on this day in 1999. Cork become All-Ireland champions by beating kilkenny 0-13 to 0-12.

'A lot of us laid to rest an awful lot of ghosts out there. I've been tempted to say this all year: we haven't gone away, you know.' Cork manager Jimmy Barry-Murphy on winning the 1999 All-Ireland Senior hurling final on this day.

Henry Shefflin scores a point from a free on the forty-seventh minute of their All-Ireland Senior hurling encounter with Cork on this day in 2004 to put them ahead 0-8 to 0-9. It was to be Kilkenny's last score of the game with Cork scoring the next nine without reply to win the game 0-17 to 0-9.

September 13th

‘It doesn’t matter who wins or who loses. What we saw today was a clear expression of what Ireland is all about. We can put on a show like that and show the world that we are unique and that we are part of the wider world. Nobody who watched that today could possibly believe that it was anything but Irish. The finish was marvellous.’ Minister for Sport, Jim McDaid TD on this day in 1997 on a thrilling hurling final that finished Clare 0-20, Tipperary 2-13.

On this day in 1925 Sligo had to play Roscommon six times in the Connacht Senior football championship before winning, 2-3 to 0-2. The delay eventually led to Connacht Champions Galway being awarded the All-Ireland title.

Brian Whelehan recovering from flu scored 1-6 in the All-Ireland Senior hurling final on this day in 1998. Whelehan’s goal in the sixty-seventh minute and a penalty that went over the bar from DJ Carey gave Offaly a 2-16 to 1-13 win.

September 14th

Galway win their first All-Ireland Senior hurling final on this day in 1924 playing for the much delayed 1923 championship. Limerick had originally refused to meet the fixture until all Republican prisoners held in the Civil War were released. Limerick and Kerry were at one stage suspended from the association at a time when the association came under serious strain. In a special Congress it was agreed to lift the suspensions and go ahead with the finals. The final score was 7-3 to 4-5.

Cork Senior Hurling titles: 1890, 1892, 1893, 1894, 1902, 1903, 1919, 1926, 1928, 1929, 1931, 1941, 1942, 1943, 1944, 1946, 1952, 1953, 1954, 1966, 1970, 1976, 1977, 1978, 1984, 1986, 1990, 1999, 2004, 2005.

Martin Comerford of Kilkenny scored a goal in the last five minutes of the All-Ireland Senior hurling final on this day in 2003 to give the Cats captained by DJ Carey a win over Cork, 1-14 to 1-11.

September 15th

Meath lost their second All-Ireland in a row on this day in 1991 when they were beaten by Down. At one stage Down were nine points ahead but Meath made a spirited attempt to make a comeback in the second half that included a Liam Hayes goal and finished the game 1-16 to 1-14. Down left Croke Park with their record of never being beaten in the All-Ireland final intact. 60,500 spectators had turned up to watch the game compared to the record 90,556 who watched Down and Offaly in 1961.

Jack Flavin won an All-Ireland with Kerry in 1937 and another with Galway in 1938.

Mayo, who at one stage led the All-Ireland Senior football final by six points, on this day in 1996 were eventually forced to a replay by a late Meath revival and Colm Coyle goal. Meath won the replay in which Colm Coyle again was of note but for a red card instead of a goal.

September 16th

The US 'Invasion' begins on this day in 1888 when GAA athletes and hurlers set sail to New York on The Wisconsin to promote Gaelic games in the States. Poor planning resulted in lower turnouts than expected and left the GAA in a tough financial position at a crucial stage of its development. It would take the record attendances between Kildare and Kerry in two replays in 1905 before the organisation was back on sound financial ground, that and the agreement of patrons like Michael Davitt to waive all claim to subscriptions raised for the trip. The fact that many of the athletes remained in the States was a further blow.

Kerry, captained by Tim Kennelly, beat Dublin for the second year running in the All-Ireland Senior football final on this day in 1978. The final score was 3-13 to 1-8. Two of the Kerry goals were scored by Mike Sheehy, the second a penalty, and the game also saw Páidí Ó Sé sent off in the second half.

September 17th

'Everything that could go wrong did go wrong really. There were awful mistakes made by everyone. We started off by not winning the breaks around midfield and carried on then. The defence was getting bombarded and it was only a matter of time before they collapsed and that's exactly what happened.' Cork captain Derek Kavanagh on their loss in the All-Ireland final to Kerry 3-13 to 1-9 on this day in 2007.

Cork managed by Billy Morgan appeared in their third All-Ireland Senior football final in a row on this day in 1989 having lost the previous two. They made no mistakes this time, picking up Sam for the first time in sixteeen years, by beating John O'Mahony's Mayo by 0-17 to 1-11.

Dublin beat Tyrone with the help of a Charlie Redmond goal on this day in 1995 to win the All-Ireland Senior football title, 1-10 to 0-12. Peter Canavan scored all but one of the Tyrone scores and Redmond the goal hero was sent off.

September 18th

71,988 fans witnessed a bruising encounter between Dublin and Galway in the All-Ireland Senior football final in Croke Park on this day in 1983. Three players had already been sent off when a melee broke out in the tunnel as the two teams headed to the dressing room at half time, an incident that left Galwayman Brian Talty suffering from a blow to the head and unable to rejoin play in the second half. Another sending off in the second half for Ciaran Duff for a wild kick that just missed the head of Galway defender, Pat O'Neill, left the Dubs with only twelve men against fourteen. Despite this Dublin managed to hold on to win the game 1-10 to 1-8, the goal coming from Barney Rock at the start of the first half. No doubt the very poor weather on the day caused some of the friction but the GAA quickly moved to punish the offenders with Ciaran Duff receiving the longest suspension, one year, and Kevin Heffernan the Dublin Manager receiving a three month ban for incursions on to the pitch.

Kevin O'Brien the Wicklow footballer won his county's first ever All Star award in 1990.

September 19th

Laois captained by Dick Millar won the first ever National league football title on this day in 1926 when they beat Dublin 2-1 to 1-0 at Barretts Park in New Ross.

'We all know in Clare that he doesn't like us.' Clare hurling team manager Ger Loughnane, taking umbrage with the All-Ireland hurling final analysis provided by Eamonn Cregan on RTE, speaking on this day in 1997.

Seamus Darby of Offaly scored 'that goal' on this day in the 1982 Senior football title to prevent Kerry winning a record five championships in a row.

Derry win their first All-Ireland Senior football final on this day in 1993 when they beat Cork 1-14 to 2-8.

September 20th

Michael Cusack, the founding father of the GAA, was born on this day in 1847 into a Gaelic speaking household in Carron, County Clare.

Donegal make their first ever appearance in an All-Ireland Senior football final on this day in 1992 and go on to lift Sam for the first time beating Dublin 0-18 to 0-14.

Kerry win their second four-in-a-row All-Ireland Senior football title on this day in 1981, becoming the first team to do so. In the semi-final Kerry had kept Mayo scoreless in the second half and a late goal from Jack O'Shea in the final put the game beyond Offaly, 1-12 to 0-8.

Meath appeared in their first All-Ireland Senior football final since 1970 on this day in 1987. Colm O'Rourke scored Meath's only goal to help secure a win against Cork, 1-14 to 0 11.

September 21st

In 1951 Mayo retained the All-Ireland Senior football title against Meath, which they had won the previous year when beating Louth. On both of those occasions the Mayo left corner back and captain was Sean Flanagan. His son Dermot played in the same position in the Senior football final in 1996 but this time Mayo failed to win.

Mike Sheehy, Denis ‘Ogie’ Moran, Páidí Ó Sé, Pat Spillane and Ger Power all win their eighth All-Ireland Senior football medals on this day in 1986 when they beat Tyrone, who were making their first appearance in a final, 2-15 to 1-10.

Cork win the 1919 All-Ireland Senior hurling final on this day in 1920, delayed by the ongoing war in the country. They beat Dublin 6-4 to 2-4 wearing their famous red jerseys in a hurling final for the first time. Jimmy Kennedy scored four goals in the first half to guarantee the win, outscoring the whole Dublin team.

September 22nd

Galway lose to Dublin in the All-Ireland Senior football final on this day in 1963, 1-9 to 0-10. It was to be the first of four appearances in a row for Galway who more happily went on to win three All-Irelands in a row, the first time any Connacht team had done so, and bringing a fourth All-Ireland medal to Galway player Mattie McDonagh.

Louth win their first All-Ireland Senior football final in forty-five years on this day in 1957. A late goal from Seán Cunningham was the winner for Louth against Cork, 1-9 to 1-7.

Seán O'Neill scored in the sixth minute against Kerry on this day in 1968 to help Down to an All-Ireland Senior football final win, 2-12 to 1-13. Down had led by six points going into the final two minutes with Kerry getting a consolation goal from Brendan Lynch just before the whistle.

September 23rd

Cork won the 1973 All-Ireland Senior football final on this day beating Galway in the highest scoring game of the eighty-minute finals that were in place from 1970 to 1974. The final score was 3-17 to 2-13.

Kerry win the All-Ireland Senior football final on this day, the centenary year of the GAA, in 1984 beating Dublin 0-14 to 1-6. Kerry would go on to win three in a row but then not win another All-Ireland final until 1997.

Cork win their first All-Ireland Senior football final in thirty four years on this day in 1945. A Cork side containing Jack Lynch beat Cavan 2-5 to 0-7, the goals coming from Mick Tubridy and Derry Beckett.

September 24th

'Kerry will always come back. We've dusted ourselves down before and we'll do it again.' Tomás Ó Sé, Kerry footballer, on the resilience of his team, after they lost to Tyrone in the 2008 All-Ireland football final.

A record 90,556 spectators turns up at Croke Park on this day in 1961 to watch Down win Sam for the second time in a row. They beat Offaly, 3-6 to 2-8. It was Offaly's first ever appearance in a final.

Cavan become the first Ulster team to win an All-Ireland Senior football final on this day in 1933, it was also the first time the final involved an Ulster Connacht clash. Cavan were favourites having beaten the four-in-a-row Kerry side in the semi-final and two goals in the first half sent them on their way, one coming from Jim Smith who became the first Cavan captain to lift Sam.

September 25th

Down, known as the Mourne County, won their first All-Ireland Senior football final on this day in 1960 when they beat Kerry 2-10 to 0-8. 90,556 turn up at Croke Park the following year to watch them do it again against Offaly. They have added another three since.

Kerry captained by Joe Barrett win their fourth All-Ireland football title in a row on this day in 1932 beating Mayo 2-7 to 2-4 in front of 25,816 spectators at Croke Park. Kerry were the second team to achieve this, Wexford having done so in 1918.

Meath win their first All-Ireland Senior title on this day in 1949. Bill Halpenny scored Meath's goal to help them to a 1-10 to 1-6 victory over Cavan. It had taken Meath three games to get past Louth in the Leinster semi-final in the same year, games that had generated a big interest in the winning Meath side and a record 79,460 turned up to watch the All-Ireland final.

September 26th

Offaly, known as the Faithful County, won their first All-Ireland Senior football title on this day in 1971 when they beat Galway 1-14 to 2-8. In 1972 they repeated the success when they beat Kerry in a replay of the final. They have four Senior football titles and three Senior hurling titles in total.

Galway beat Kerry on this day in 1965 to win their second All-Ireland in a row against the Kingdom, they would beat Meath for three-in-a-row the next year. The final score was 0-12 to 0-9 with three players being sent off.

Meath won their second All-Ireland Senior football title on this day in 1954 having been in three out of the five finals since they had won their first in 1949. Tom Moriarty scored Meath's only goal in the twentieth minute to set them up for the win, 1-13 to 1-7.

September 27th

‘We had our Viagra at half-time.’ Galway footballer Niall Finnegan on their All-Ireland Senior football final win over Kildare on this day in 1998 when they won 1-14 to 1-10 having trailed at half time 1-5 to 0-5.

‘The qualifier system has made the All-Ireland harder to win but expectations in Kerry havn’t reduced.’ John O’Keefe the former Kerry Manager on this day in 2003.

Galway won the first of three All-Ireland Senior football titles in a row on this day in 1964 beating Kerry 0-15 to 0-10. They would not concede a goal in any of the three finals. Tragically former county captain Mick Donnellan died of a heart attack while watching the game in Croke Park, his son John was captain that day. John Donnellan’s son Michael would also go on to win an All-Ireland Senior title on this day in 1998 when Galway beat Kildare in the final.

September 28th

‘When Oisín McConville cut inside and fired that goal to the net in the second half, the X-factor was unleashed upon us. A hundred years of oppression, of f**king helicopters, of jack booted troops kicking them when they were down, the lot.’ Páidí Ó Sé on this day in 2002 talking about Kerry’s loss to Armagh in the All-Ireland Senior Football final 1-12 to 0-14.

Kildare won their second All-Ireland Senior title when they beat Galway comprehensively on this day in 1919. Galway were held to the same one point score they had managed on their last appearance, in the home final of 1900, losing 2-5 to 0-1.

Dublin won their third three-in-a-row All-Ireland Senior football final on this day in 1924, playing for the delayed 1923 championship. Beating a Kerry team made up of pro and anti-treaty players, 1-5 to 1-3.

September 29th

Meath beat Mayo in the replay of the All-Ireland Senior football final on this day in 1996. In a game that saw Colm Coyle and Liam McHale sent off after a mass brawl Meath punished Mayo for not finishing the Royal county off when they had a six point lead in the first game. Trevor Giles scored a penalty and Tommy Dowd got Meath's other goal to win 2-9 to 1-11.

In the 1942 Leinster Senior football semi-final the referee in the match between Carlow and Offaly blew for full time ten minutes early. After threats from spectators he tried to restart the match but Offaly refused to continue and were suspended for six months.

'Ah, I took the chance and put the hurl up and flicked it in the net. Just one of those things.' DJ Carey on the memorable goal he scored in the 2002 All-Ireland Senior hurling final when they beat Clare.

September 30th

Limerick win a replayed All-Ireland Senior hurling final on this day in 1934, a game in which Dave Clohessy of Limerick scored four goals. Unsurprisingly Limerick with the great Mick Mackey in the side went on to win 5-2 to 2-6, their first All-Ireland since lifting the first Liam McCarthy cup in 1921.

Offaly play at St. Brendan's Park, Birr with a capacity of 25,000.

Kildare appeared in their third All-Ireland Senior football final in a row on this day in 1928 beating Cavan 2-6 to 2-5, making it two wins out of three. They were the first to lift the new Sam Maguire cup. While Kildare went on to appear in their fourth All-Ireland final in a row the following year, which resulted in a loss to Kerry, they have yet to add another All-Ireland Senior football title.

October 1st

'There were no fights among the spectators and all true Irishmen know that you cannot have a hurling match without a fight.' Daily Mail report on a match in London on this day in 1921.

Dublin won the All-Ireland Senior football final of 1908, on this day in 1909, by beating London at the Jones' Road ground, 1-10 to 0-4. However, at that stage they had already been knocked out of the 1909 championship. Louth had beaten them three weeks earlier, 1-7 to 1-11, on the 12th of September 1909.

'A bet of 300 guineas, a cold dinner and a Ball at night for the Ladies, to be hurled for on Friday 9th inst., by 21 married men and 21 bachelors, on the Green of Ardfinnan in the County of Tipperary.' Notice in the Cork Evening Post in 1769.

October 2nd

Austin Stack's of Kerry, formerly known as Rock Street GAA Club, was founded in 1917 but took the name of Austin Stack after his death in 1929. In 1928 the club had won its first county Senior football title. They supplied the Landers brothers, Joe Barrett, Jackie Ryan and Miko Doyle to the Kerry side who won twenty-one All-Ireland Senior medals between them. In the 1970s when they won four titles, between 1973 and 1979, they supplied Mikey Sheehy, John O'Keeffe and Ger Power to the Kerry side winning twenty-three All-Ireland medals between them.

Dick Spring, former Labour leader and Tánaiste, played hurling and football for Kerry in the 1974-5 league campaign

'Traditional values provide ballast in an era of aimlessness and disillusionment' Seamus Ó Riain, GAA President 1965.

October 3rd

A record 30,000 people turned up, on this day in 1926, to see Cork and Tipperary in a second replay of the Munster final, in Thurles. Tipperary had a player sent off in the first half and being a goal down at half time never recovered, against a team filled with players from the famous Blackrock club in Cork, 3-6 to 2-4.

Wexford play at Wexford Park with a capacity of 25,000.

'They are even more intense this year than last year, like boys who haven't been fed for two weeks. Once they got their leg in there they just kept going and going.' Tipperary's Brendan Cummins on Kilkenny's second-half semi-final display in 2003. Kilkenny went on beat Cork in the final.

October 4th

Waterford won their last All-Ireland Senior hurling final to date when they beat Kilkenny on this day in 1959 in a replay, 3-12 to 1-10. 77,825 spectators turned up to see the replay given the quality of the hurling in the first game. The first half finished Kilkenny three points behind but they only managed to score two points in the second half to Waterford's seven.

'The vast majority of the best athletes in Ireland are nationalists. These gentlemen should take the matter in hand at once, and draft laws for the guidance of the promoters of meetings in Ireland next year.' Michael Cusack in the United Ireland newspaper 1884.

Peter McDermott who captained the 1954 All-Ireland Senior football champions Meath and won an earlier title with the side when they won their first Senior title in 1949 was also the trainer for the Down side that won their first All-Ireland Senior title in 1960.

October 5th

‘I likened it to the Vietnam War. Nobody back home cared that much, but the people over there did.’ Leigh Matthews Australia’s Coach on their approach to the International Rules series with Ireland, October 1998.

‘There is quite an amount of evidence that the huge increase in the number of live televised games has impacted on attendances at club competitions.’ Liam Mulvihill report to Congress.

‘The greatest game of hurling I have ever seen.’ Ger Loughnane describes the first game between two teams from the same province, in an All-Ireland Senior hurling final, in 1997 when Clare and Tipperary met. Liam Cahill and Eugene O’Neill of Tipperary scored a goal each in the last ten minutes to draw the game but a late point from Jamesie O’Connor put Clare back in the lead. John Leahy missed a late goal chance to give victory to Clare.

October 6th

At the Ulster club hurling final between Antrim team Dunloy and Lavey from Derry on this day in 1997 five players were sent off during extra time in the match, three were from Dunloy and two from Lavey. There was a pitch invasion at the end of the game, mostly of Dunloy supporters who tried to attack the referee, John Anthony Gribben from Down.

Niall Quinn played for the Dublin hurlers in the 1983 All-Ireland Minor final before going on to a successful career with Arsenal, Manchester City and Sunderland.

'Our Irish temperament would appear to be more controllable in the hands of a referee who is familiar with members of the team.' Dick Fitzgerald, in his book 'How to Play Gaelic Football ' published in 1914.

October 7th

Seán Purcell of Tuam Stars in Galway, who secured ten Senior county medals with the club, won his first and only All-Ireland Senior football medal on this day in 1956 when the tribesmen beat Cork 2-13 to 3-7. The final had been delayed because of a polio outbreak in Cork. He was picked for both the Football team of the Century in 1984 to mark the centenary of the GAA and the Football Team of the Millennium in 1999.

Dublin win their second title in a row on this day in 1923, playing for the delayed 1922 championship. Galway making their third unsuccessful appearance in a final were the opposition losing 0-6 to 0-4, an improvement on the single scores they had only managed in each of their last two appearances.

'Play every match as if it was your last, but play well enough to ensure it isn't.' Jack Lynch

October 8th

'The fact is the GAA has given far more to the Exchequer than it has received - by way of taxes that have accrued as a result of its investment in Croke Park and other grounds throughout the country, not to mention the employment and revenue generated by its activities.' Danny Lynch GAA PRO on this day in 2004.

John Doyle of Holycross club in Tipperary became the second hurler after Christy Ring to win eight All-Ireland Senior hurling titles. He won his first Senior All-Ireland in 1949 at the age of 19 making it three in a row with wins for Tipperary in 1950 and 1951. He was still playing when Tipperary won their next title seven years later in 1958 and added another four, his last win came in 1965. During his playing career he never missed a championship match for the Premier county. He retired after Kilkenny beat Tipperary in the 1967 final, depriving him of a record making ninth medal. He was named in the Hurling Team of the Millennium at right full back.

October 9th

'I think he gave all the answers. Every time he got the ball, he was electric. Nobody could mark him. Inside, up in the air, kicking points, giving passes, getting goals, he was unbelievable.' Kieran Donaghy of Kerry discusses Colm 'the Gooch' Cooper's talents.

On this day in 1988 Meath, playing Cork for the second year in a row in the All-Ireland football final, beat them in an ill tempered replay despite Gerry McEntee being sent off in the sixth minute, 0-13 to 0-12.

Martin O'Neill played Gaelic football in Derry before going on to a successful career with Nottingham Forest as a footballer and Celtic and Aston Villa as a manager.

October 10th

A meeting on this day in 1885 instructs that posts be erected twenty-one yards to either side of the goals for the scoring of points on a trial basis. While the trial is deemed a success a goal still outscores any number of points for the next seven years.

Roscommon are known as the Rossies or the Sheep stealers and have two Senior All-Ireland titles in football.

'The team wasn't fit in '96, wasn't ready for the championship. Three weeks before, I was doing three-hour sessions to get them ready and that's crazy. I now know an unfit, fresh team is better than a fit, tired one.' Michael McNamara, Clare's hurling trainer in 1995 when they won their first All-Ireland since 1914, on one of the reasons why they failed against Limerick in the 1996 Munster final.

October 11th

‘We tell the Irish people to take the management of their games into their hands, to encourage and promote in every way every form of athletics which is peculiarly Irish, and to remove with one sweep everything foreign and iniquitous in the present system.’ Michael Cusack in the United Ireland newspaper on this day in 1884.

The 1931 All-Ireland Senior hurling replay played on this day in 1931 between Cork and Kilkenny is often discussed as possibly the greatest game of hurling ever. In a first half that saw a goal from the great Blackrock and Cork player Eudie Coughlan and a half time score of 2-4 to 1-3, Cork only managed to score one point in the second half to force another replay. After the replay a motion before Central Council, which was defeated, suggested the honours be split between the teams. In the second replay Cork were the winners, 5-8 to 3-4.

October 12th

'You probably think I am a respected man in this town. There are people in this town, boy, that think I am locked up the red house on the hill and only let out to hurl on Sunday.' Christy Ring.

Tipperary play at Semple Stadium, Thurles with a capacity of 53,000. The ground is named in honour of local man Tom Semple who was involved in the original purchase of the ground for the GAA in 1910 and who also won two All-Ireland Senior medals for Tipperary. The first Munster hurling final held there was in 1914.

'You dream of winning every ball and every contest when you are in a final but it never turns out like that. Except last week for Kilkenny.' Seán Óg Ó hAilpín the Cork hurler on Kilkenny's performance in the 2008 All-Ireland Senior hurling final when they scored 3-30 against Waterford.

October 13th

The Leinster Council is formed on this day in 1900. The first president is Alderman James Nowlan of Kilkenny and the first secretary is Matt Hanrahan of Wexford.

Laois win their first ever Leinster Senior football final on this day in 1889 when they beat Louth at Inchicore. Portlaoise, represented Laois, and Louth were represented by Newtown Blues with a final score of 0-3 to 0-2. Laois were beaten in the final a week later when they failed to score against Tipperary.

'Irish football is a great game and worth going a long way to see when played on a fairly laid out ground and under proper rules. Many old people say just hurling exceeded it as a trial of men. I would not care to see either game now as the rules stand at present. I may say there are no rules and therefore those games are often dangerous.' Maurice Davin on this day in 1884

October 14th

The Munster Council is formed on this day in 1900. The first president is Patrick McGrath of Tipperary and the first secretary is P.J. Hayes of Limerick. However controversy abounds and a centrally recognised council is not formed until June the 30th 1901 when Richard Cummins of Tipperary is president and Thomas Dooley of Cork is the agreed secretary.

Only Fermanagh and Wicklow have failed to win a Senior provincial title in either code. Fermanagh however did reach the All-Ireland Senior football semi-final in 2004 where they lost out to Mayo.

'I felt myself that everything Kerry football stood for was on the line. Everything we'd achieved in the last four or five years, and everything we'd achieved in the last 100 years, was riding on that seventy minutes of football. It was that fear of losing to Cork that was driving us.' Paul Galvin of Kerry proves that local rivalry is bigger than the national stage, as Kerry beat Cork in the 2007 All-Ireland final.

October 15th

Mayo win their first ever National League football final on this day in 1934 when they beat Dublin, 2-4 to 1-5. Mayo would go on to win a record six titles in a row.

Irish rugby international Moss Keane won three Sigerson Cup medals with UCC.

'It is that sense of allegiance to something permanent and enduring that has always been our strength. Our rules derive not only from a desire to organise health-giving exercise but from a determination to defend the national values, traditions and aims. That is what has given an enduring vitality to the work of the Gaelic Athletic Association.' Dan O'Rourke, GAA President 1962

October 16th

'There was a grand Hurling Match in the neighbourhood of Gort in the county for the considerable sum of Money between the counties of Galway and Clare, the Hurlers of the latter made a very handsome appearance.' Report on a proposed hurling game in a newspaper on this day in 1759.

The Tailteann Games discontinued by the GAA in 1932 saw a peak of interest when in 1924 the US Olympic team stopped in Dublin to compete in the events.

Meath play at Páirc Tailteann, Navan with a capacity of 28,000.

'It chews away at me, yes, I am gutted. Forty-six years and we still haven't done it.' Former Mayo manager John Maughan makes his feelings clear.

October 17th

Kerry met Kildare in the All-Ireland Senior football final in 1926. The sides could not be separated and the game went to a replay after a 1-3 to 0-6 score with the Kingdom's Bill Gorman scoring the only goal of the game in the final minutes. One of the Kerry stars of the day, twenty-two year old Johnny Murphy, took ill and missed the replay, played on this day in 1926, which Kerry won 1-4 to 0-4. Sadly Johnny Murphy did not recover from his illness and died a few days after the replay.

The old Liam McCarthy cup was replaced with a newer model in 1992. Kilkenny were the first winners beating Cork 3-10 to 1-12 in the final.

'Yesterday, Tuesday, a hurling match took place in the Phoenix Park, which was honoured with the presence of Her Excellency, the countess of Westmoreland, and several of the nobility and gentry, besides a vast concourse of spectators.' Report in the Hibernian Journal on this day in 1792.

October 18th

New York, in their Golden Jubilee year, won their second National League football title on this day in 1964 beating the visiting Dublin team 2-12 to 1-13 at the Gaelic Park in New York. Dublin had been reigning All-Ireland champions when they won the home final against Down back in May but went into the game having lost their Leinster title to Meath during the summer. New York on the other hand had carried out a world tour to celebrate their Golden Jubilee and the exiles surprised all to add another element to their celebrations.

Clare, known as the Banner County, have won three All-Irelands Senior hurling titles. They won their first on this day in 1914 when they beat Laois 5-1 to 1-0. Laois failed to register a single score in the first half. Clare, trained by Micheál Ó Hehir's father Andy, were represented by Quin while Laois were represented by Kilcotton. Laois would reappear and win the next final in 1915 but Clare would not win another final until 1995.

October 19th

Galway won their first All-Ireland in Senior football in 1925 by winning the Connacht final. Semi-finalists Cavan and Kerry were both disqualified. Mayo had been picked to represent Connacht, due to that province's much delayed championship, had beaten Wexford the other semi-finalists but had yet to play the Connacht final. Galway won that final 1-5 to 1-3 with a late goal from Michael 'Knacker' Walsh and were on this day declared the All-Ireland champions, the day after the Connacht final.

'The real problem with the foot-and-mouth epidemic, Pat, is that you didn't get it.' Ted Walsh to Pat Spillane.

'Our games were in a most grievous condition until the brave and patriotic men who started the Gaelic Athletic Association took their revival in hand. The instantaneous and extraordinary success which attended their efforts fills me with great hope for Ireland's future.' Douglas Hyde 1892.

October 20th

On this day in 1889 Tipperary, represented by Bohercrowe, beat Laois, represented by Maryborough, to win their first All-Ireland Senior football title. The score was 3-6 to 0-0. At that time a goal outscored any number of points so this game would have been scored three goals nil; goals were only given a point value three years later.

Dublin win the 1906 All-Ireland Senior football final, played in Athy, on this day in 1907. They beat Cork, represented by Lees, 0-5 to 0-4. Kickhams represent Dublin in a final for the third time, winning two out of three. In an attempt to clear the backlog of fixtures this is the second All-Ireland final played in less than five months.

Sligo known as Yeats' County, the Zebras or Magpies have a solitary All-Ireland title in Junior football. In 1922 they had reached the All-Ireland final but were forced to replay the Connacht final after an objection from Galway and lost by two points.

October 21st

'The first one was in Cork and straight away, Mick Lyons was carted off. My fella didn't hit me but nearly everyone else drew a slap on their man.' Eoin 'Bomber' Liston on the first International Rules test played on this day in 1984. The Australians won the first series 2-1 but the series was remembered most for the fighting, with three players being sent off in the final test in Croke Park.

'We should not even entertain a motion relating to the foreign games until the National Flag flies over the 32 counties of a free and undivided Ireland.' Motion from Tyrone before the 1947 GAA Congress.

American football player Tom Furlong who played with the New York Giants and the Atlanta Falcons was first an inter-county player for Offaly.

October 22nd

Only a month after winning the All-Ireland football final of 1933 Cavan were beaten by Meath, on this day in 1933, in the National League football final, 0-10 to 1-6.

'No one will expect onlookers unduly to withhold their enthusiasm and ardour on the occasion of big matches, and Irish human nature seems to revel in a good shout, whether of triumph or reproach.' Dick Fitzgerald in his 1914 instructional manual 'How to Play Gaelic Football.'

Patrick Kielty played Minor football with Down,winning an All-Ireland medal, before going on to a successful career as a comedian.

The Croke cups awarded for the National League were originally for a separate competition called the Croke Cups between 1896 and 1915.

October 23rd

'I feel lucky to be a part of all of this. I was about to quit two years ago but I was encouraged to go on by the very nature of Liam Griffin's approach. I knew he was something special.' George O'Connor of Wexford explains why he decided to stay playing inter county hurling for his seventeenth championship in 1996, winning an All-Ireland Senior hurling medal in the process.

Bobby Beggs wins an All-Ireland Senior football medal with Dublin in 1942 when they beat Galway 1-10 to 1-8. Four years earlier on this day he had won an All-Ireland with the very same Galway when they beat Kerry after a replay.

Irish rugby international Keith Wood played under-16 hurling with County Tipperary in 1988.

October 24th

On this day in 1948 Cavan and Cork met in the replay of the National league football final, the first game played on the 20th of June was interrupted by the championship which Cavan had won for the second year in a row. Cavan captained by John Joe O'Reilly were convincing winners 5-9 to 2-8.

Laois won their first All-Ireland Senior hurling final on this day in 1915 when they beat Cork 6-2 to 4-1. Laois who had been badly beaten in the previous year's final drafted in help in the form of Dick 'Drug' Walsh from Kilkenny. Walsh arranged for practice games against his old side in the weeks leading up to the final and it obviously paid off for a team who had not scored in the first half of the previous year's final.

Cork back in the All-Ireland Senior hurling final after seven years made no mistakes when they beat Kilkenny 4-6 to 2-0 on a snow covered Croke Park on this day in 1926.

October 25th

‘It is a hard place to get back to, a final, and it’s very satisfying that we are there again. We are not setting the world on fire. We are playing some nice football and some ordinary football and getting the right results at this time.’ Mickey Harte of Tyrone discusses the challenge of getting to another All-Ireland final in 2008.

Wembley Stadium London was hired by the GAA between 1958 and 1976 for an annual festival, which saw a record attendance of 42,500 in 1963.

The Artane Boys Band first performed at the All-Ireland finals in 1886, which were actually for the delayed 1885 championships.

Irish international soccer player Shane Long played Minor hurling for Tipperary.

October 26th

Tipperary become the second team to win the All Ireland hurling final three times in a row, Cork having done it six years earlier, when they beat London on this day in 1902 for the delayed 1900 championship. London were in the competition representing a fifth province and 'home' finals were played before London entered the competition for the final proper for the next four years.

Sam Maguire appears at the All-Ireland Senior football final for the first time on this day in 1902, this time it was the man after whom the All-Ireland football trophy is named. Maguire was playing for London in the final proper against Tipperary, who had allowed Galway only one score in the home final 2-17 to 0-1. London were no match for the Premier men who, playing for the 1900 championship, won the game 3-7 to 0-2. The Sam Maguire trophy first appeared at a final in 1928.

October 27th

In a letter sent out on this day in 1884 Michael Cusack called a meeting in Thurles 'for the formation of a Gaelic Association for the preservation of and cultivation of our national pastimes.'

Michael Donnellan of Galway won an All-Ireland Senior football title in 1998 and became the third generation of his family to win a title with Galway. His father was part of the winning team in 1964, 1965, 1966 and his Grandfather in 1925.

Kilkenny have thirty one Senior Hurling titles after wining the 2008 final to put them one ahead of Cork their record is as follows: 1904, 1905, 1907, 1909, 1911, 1912, 1913, 1922, 1932, 1933, 1935, 1939, 1947, 1957, 1963, 1967, 1969, 1972, 1974, 1975, 1979, 1982, 1983, 1992, 1993, 2000, 2002, 2003, 2006, 2007 and 2008.

October 28th

Dublin beat Tipperary to win their first All-Ireland Senior hurling title since 1889 on this day in 1917. Two brothers from Tipperary played in the final but one on either side, Stephen Hackett for Tipperary and Martin Hackett for Dublin. Joe Phelan score three goals for Dublin, represented by Collegians, to help his side beat Tipperary the reigning champions, represented by Boherlahan, 5-4 to 4-2. This was the Premier county's second All-Ireland in one year having played the delayed 1916 final ten months earlier.

'If we're relegated, we would have to end up as defeated Leinster finalists to get into the qualifiers. We could beat Westmeath and Offaly and then lose narrowly to Dublin or Louth in the semi-final, but wouldn't be allowed in, yet Westmeath and Offaly would. That's ridiculous.' Luke Dempsey the Longford football manager points out some concerns with the qualifier system in advance of the 2008 Congress where it was agreed Division four teams would no longer be excluded from the first round qualifiers.

October 29th

Tipperary beat Dublin, 3-16 to 3-8, on this day in 1907 to win the delayed 1906 All-Ireland Senior hurling final. Tipperary were on their way to their seventh title when Paddy Riordan scored within seconds of the throw in for the Premier county. Eleven of the Dublin team that day were originally from Tipperary.

'Teams would have been on their way, supporters were staying in town. It wouldn't have been feasible.' Danny Lynch PRO of the GAA explains why the Kilkenny game against Waterford went ahead in the 1998 championship and wasn't postponed after the Omagh bombing.

The Rules Today

In hurling the ball may be struck with the hurley when it is on the ground, in the air, tossed from the hand or lifted with the hurley.

October 30th

Meath were Leinster Senior football champions for twenty minutes in 1911 when the final was awarded to them when Kilkenny failed to show. When Kilkenny did show the game went ahead after heated discussion, which was won by Kilkenny after a replay.

Tipperary are known as the Premier county and have twenty-five Senior All-Ireland hurling titles and four Senior football titles. They won their first All-Ireland hurling Final in 1887 and contested and won the first Senior hurling final held at Jones' Road, now Croke Park.

The Rules Today

In football the ball has to weigh between 370 and 425 grams and have a circumference of between 69 and 74 centimetres. In hurling the sliotar must weigh between 110 and 120 grams and have a circumference of between 69 and 72 centimetres not including the rim.

October 31st

In the 1950 Munster Senior hurling final Tipperary beat Cork, 2-7 to 3-11. The game is remembered equally for the continual incursions onto the Fitzgerald Stadium pitch by mainly Cork fans who targeted the Tipperary goalkeeper Tony Reddan for particular attention. At the end of the game he had to be smuggled out of the ground. It was also Jack Lynch's last game for Cork.

Tipperary finished the 1960 All-Ireland Senior hurling final with only 12 men when some players left thinking a free in the last minute, that resulted in a pitch invasion, was the final whistle. After the pitch was cleared Wexford won by 2-15 to 0-11 points.

'The GAA intends to delete Rule 21 from its official guide when the effective steps are taken to implement the amended structures and policing arrangements envisaged in the British-Irish peace agreement.' Danny Lynch, GAA PRO 1998.

November 1st

The GAA is founded on this day in 1884 in a meeting in the billiard room of Miss Haye's Commercial Hotel, Thurles. Those in attendance were Maurice Davin, Michael Cusack, John Wyse Power, John McKay, P.J. O'Ryan, J.K. Bracken and Thomas St. George McCarthy.

Kerry earn a replay of the All-Ireland Senior football final against Wexford on this day in 1914. The Kingdom had been down five points at one stage but staged a remarkable comeback in the second half with a Paddy Breen goal. It was the second meeting of the sides in a final, after Kerry had won the previous year, while Kerry proved too much in the replay it was obvious Wexford were becoming a force in football.

The Rules Today

The referee cannot permit the wearing of a helmet in football.

November 2nd

Kilkenny win their first ever three-in-a-row when they win the All-Ireland Senior hurling title on this day in 1913. In the first final played with fifteen-a-side Kilkenny beat Tipperary, who scored only one point in the second half, 2-4 to 1-2. Kilkenny would not win another three-in-row despite their continued success until 2008.

'In short the Offaly defence smothered the Kilkenny attackers and their lack of height told in the end.' Eamonn Cregan explains how Offaly won the 1998 hurling final.

The Rules Today

In football and hurling the scoring space is formed by two goalposts, at the centre of each endline, which must be a height of not less than seven metres above ground level and be 6.5 metres apart. A crossbar is fixed to the goalposts at a standard height of 2.5 metres above the ground and can be rectangular or secular in cross section.

November 3rd

Dublin win their first All-Ireland Senior hurling title when they beat Clare 5-1 to 1-6 on this day in 1889. Dublin were represented by Kickams while Tulla represented Clare at Inchicore in front of a crowd estimated at over a thousand. At that time a goal was worth five points and outscored any number of points so what looks like a seven point victory was actually a twenty point margin.

Antrim appear in their second All-Ireland Senior football final in a row on this day in 1912. Having disposed of Kerry in the semi-final, despite having a player sent off early in the second half, Antrim proved they deserved their place in the final. Leading for most of the game Antrim were over taken by a late flurry from Louth and lost their second final, 1-7 to 1-2. It would be their last appearance in the final to date.

November 4th

‘Yer man did everything but take the shirt and togs off him. I’ve held my tongue a long time on referees but I tell you, in a tight game like that, where people’s lives and careers are sorted out, that he didn’t give a fourteen-yard free there was unbelievable.’ Joe Kernan the Armagh manager expresses some dissatisfaction with the referee.

‘People go on about Clare’s heart. I can tell you one thing, Kilkenny won’t be beaten for heart.’ Kilkenny hurler Andy Comerford before the 2002 All-Ireland final with Clare, the Cats won 2-20 0-19.

The Rules Today

In football and hurling a team should consist of fifteen players but a county committee may reduce the number for a non-championship game. A team can start with thirteen players but should have fielded fifteen, inclusive of players ordered off or retired injured, by the start of the second half.

November 5th

Footballer Glenn Ryan who made his debut for Kildare against Louth in 1991 did not miss a championship game for his county until the Leinster semi-final in 2001.

'I have heard every excuse for being late for training. The best of all was the player who told me he was late because the wheel fell off his mobile home.' Eugene McGee, Offaly Manager.

The Rules Today

In football and hurling players may tackle an opponent in possession of the ball or if both players are moving in the same direction to play the ball. Provided the opponent has at least one foot on the ground, a player may make a side-to-side charge. In football the ball can't be wrestled from the hands of an opponent who has caught it but can be knocked from his hands by flicking it with the open hand.

November 6th

‘The selectors got it completely wrong. The whole thing was a shambles.’ Former Kilkenny hurler Eddie O’Connor on what went wrong in the 1998 All-Ireland Senior hurling final when the Cats lost to Offaly.

‘In my day, we had a few farmers, a few fishermen and a college boy to take the frees.’ Paddy ‘Bawn’ Brosnan.

The Rules Today

When the ball is on the ground in football it can be played by any part of the body other than the hand. An exception to this is when a player is knocked down or falls and the ball in his hand touches the ground, the player may fist or palm the ball away and any score achieved by such will stand. The goalkeeper may also handle the ball on the ground inside his small rectangle. Picking up from the ground by use of the knee is not allowed.

November 7th

Jim Byrne of Wexford kicks a goal direct from a free kick, over thirty yards out, in the All-Ireland Senior football final on this day in 1915 to help Wexford beat Kerry, 2-4 to 2-1, in the first of four All-Ireland wins in a row. It was the first win for the model county since 1893 and their third final appearance in succession against Kerry.

'To me it's a job of work, to go and represent both sides. Represent the spectators if you like, but there is hardly a match that I'm not blamed, by the losers. Nobody ever says I'm agin the winners, I'm always agin the losers.' Micheál Ó Hehir.

<u>The Rules Today</u>

In hurling for a run at a free kick, side line puck or puck out, a player can go outside the boundary lines, but otherwise players must remain within the field of play.

November 8th

'Offaly were absolutely dreadful. Iarnród Eireann carry less passengers than there were there today.' Colm O'Rourke discusses Offaly's exit from the championship against Dublin in 2007.

'We had a number of instances at club and county level during the year which did serious harm to the image of our games.' Liam Mulvihill former GAA Director-General speaking in 1992.

The Rules Today

Spitting at an opponent is an aggressive foul in both hurling and football for which a player can be instantly dismissed by the referee along with such offences as involvement in a melee or using abusive language to an official. Any aggressive foul committed before a game starts or during half time also invokes instant dismissal and no substitution is allowed.

November 9th

The Connacht Council is formed on this day in 1902. The first president is Joseph McBride of Mayo and the first secretary is Frank Dorr of Roscommon.

Carlow reached their first ever Leinster Senior football final on this day in 1941. Earlier in the championship of that year it had taken four games against Wexford for them to progress. Despite that great effort, and the final being played in Carlow, Dublin won the game 4-6 to 1-4.

The Rules Today

In hurling a player can run with the sliotar balanced on, or hopping on his hurley. A player can catch the sliotar, play it on his hurley and bring it back on his hand once. A player who has not caught the sliotar can play it from the hurley to his hand twice. The sliotar can be struck with the hand, kicked, or lifted off the ground with the feet.

November 10th

Tyrone known as the O'Neill County or the Red Hand have three Senior All-Ireland football titles winning their first in 2003 when they beat fellow Ulstermen Armagh by three points. In 2008 they played in the first final between two teams that had come through the qualifier system, beating Kerry 1-15 to 0-14.

'It's going to take a long while to sink in but in the history books it will always be there.' Joe Kernan the Armagh manager on their first ever All-Ireland Senior title in 2002.

The Rules Today

In hurling for all free pucks, including penalties the sliotar can be lifted and hit with the hurley or struck from the ground. If the sliotar is not lifted cleanly from the ground it must be struck from the ground but if the player delays an opposing player can make a challenge.

November 11th

'You guys should enjoy this more than any game in your life. But concentrate on the next one. You'll be very sad men if you go out between now and the Leinster final.' Dublin manager Tom Carr to Kildare players who beat Dublin for the first time since 1974 in the Leinster Championship in 1998. Kildare won the Leinster title before losing out to Galway in the final.

The Rules Today

In hurling a penalty puck is awarded for an aggressive foul within the large rectangle. The penalty puck is taken form the centre point of the twenty-metre line. A free puck from the centre of the twenty-metre line is awarded for a technical foul within the large rectangle. A maximum of three defenders are allowed remain on the goal line to defend against a penalty by the opposition.

November 12th

Kerry won their first All-Ireland Senior football title on this day in 1905 by beating London 0-11 to 0-3. The game was to decide the delayed 1903 Championship. However it would be fair to say that the real All-Ireland was played out in three momentous games against Kildare in the 'home' final that drew record crowds and gate receipts that did much to improve the popularity of the GAA. The third game brought in a gate of £270 compared to a gate of £123 for the first game and both were records for the time giving the GAA a sound financial footing for the first time. The final gave first All-Ireland medals to Kingdom greats such as Dick 'Dickeen' FitzGerald and Austin Stack, the team captain.

Cork win their second All-Ireland Senior hurling final in a row when they beat London on this day in 1905, 3-16 to 1-1. It is the last year of the home final with the winners having to play London to win the title.

November 13th

Hill 16 was largely built in 1917 from the rubble of the city centre caused by the Rising in 1916 and hence got it's name but originally it is said it had been nicknamed Hill 60 after a much bombed hill on the Western front in the Great War that raged at that time. This would appear to make sense, as the Rising at that time would have not carried the iconic number 16 until some time had passed.

'Helps the stronger teams get stronger and the weaker teams get weaker.' Sean McGuinness former Antrim hurling manager on the backdoor system.

<u>The Rules Today</u>

When the ball is played over the end line and wide by the team defending that end, a free puck is awarded to the opposing team on the sixty-five-metre line, opposite wherever the ball crossed the end line.

November 14th

‘Mind will rule and muscle yield. In senate, ship and field; when we’ve skill our strength to wield, let us take our own again.’ John O’Leary, founder of the IRB, quotes Thomas Davis in his letter accepting his appointment as Patron of the GAA in 1886.

Edward Carson leader of the Ulster Unionist Party played hurling while at Trinity College Dublin where the sport was established as part of a revivalist movement in the 1850s. Trinity College Hurley Club were the first to publish a set of rules for the playing of hurling.

The Rules Today

In hurling a puck-out must be taken from the hand. If missed it can be taken from the ground or raised with the hurley and struck but not lifted into the hand again. The ball must travel thirteen metres from the puck-out before an opposing player can challenge the taker inside the twenty-metre line.

November 15th

The IRB, the secret group behind the 1916 Rising, gain a controlling position in the GAA at the National Convention, on this day in 1886, at Thurles. IRB members had been among those who had originally formed the association and this convention saw them exert a greater control over the policy within the GAA. It is however misleading to suggest the IRB decided policy, rather their members worked in various organisiations to make sure nationalist aims were progressed. Patrick Pearse was heavily involved in the organising of football and hurling competitions through his position as headmaster at Scoil Eanna. Within four months the GAA would ban members of the Crown forces from the asociation, the fact the ban was overturned in 1895 and then reintroduced after the responsible chairman was forced out shows the way in which the IRB influence was exerted.

'A referee should be like a man. For the most part they are like old women.' Billy Rackard Wexford hurler.

November 16th

Brian Cody is appointed the Kilkenny hurling manager on this day in 1998. As a player he was captain of the All-Ireland champions in 1982 winning four Senior All-Irelands in total. Added to this he won three National Leagues in 1976, '82 and '83. He was captain of an All-Ireland winning Minor team in 1972 and also on a winning Kilkenny Under-21 side in an All-Ireland final.

Cork win their first All-Ireland Senior hurling title on this day in 1890. Cork were represented by Aghabullogue, who played in their bare feet, while Castlebrdge represented Wexford. In a rough game played at Clonturk Park Wexford were leading but the game was awarded to Cork after their captain withdrew his team due to nature of the Wexford tactics. The score had stood at 2-2 to Wexford and 1-6 to Cork which at that time would have been a winning score to Wexford, given a goal outscored any number of points. This result gave Cork both the 1890 hurling title and football title, although the delayed football final would not be played for another two years.

November 17th

Kilkenny win the 1912 All-Ireland Senior hurling title on this day when they beat Cork, 2-1 to 1-3. Cork conceded a goal in the dying minutes. Their goalkeeper pulled on and missed a long speculative ball, sent in by Kilkenny player Matt Gargan, that ran over the goal line.

'It was something like five minutes - less. When you get an opportunity like that you couldn't pass it up - not a hope. It was a plus that they'd played Clare but being honest I don't think I'd have passed it up no matter what happened.' Davy Fitzgerald on the time it took him to decide to accept the Waterford job in the wake of Justin McCarthy's exit in 2008.

The Rules Today

A score will be allowed if in the opinion of the referee the ball was prevented from crossing the goal line by anyone other than a player or the referee.

November 18th

‘Until such time as Cork County Board bring in a rule that, once you come to Minor you opt for either hurling or football, in my estimation Cork are going nowhere in either hurling or football.’ Donal O’Grady former Cork manager comments on this day in 2003, Cork went on to win the All-Ireland Senior Hurling final in 2004 and again in 2005.

Waterford are known as the Crystal County, Suirsiders, the Deise or the Decies. They have two Senior All-Ireland hurling titles, winning their first in 1948 when they beat Dublin by eleven points.

The Rules Today

In football a player who is fouled may take a free kick from his hands or the ground. A fellow team member can be nominated to take the free instead. The player must indicate to the referee whether the free will be taken from the hand or ground and not change that decision.

November 19th

'Well, the ball broke between Brian and myself and fortunately it fell to me and I saw space ahead. I just decided to have a go and luckily it went in.' Waterford hurler Anthony Kirwan on scoring a goal twenty-five seconds into the second half of the 1998 Munster final.

The Galway colours of maroon and white were first introduced in the 1934 championship, prior to that year Galway had worn blue and gold.

The Rules Today

In football a penalty is awarded for an aggressive foul within the defender's large rectangle or for any foul within the small rectangle. The penalty kick is taken from the centre of the thirteen-metre line. A goalkeeper may move along his goal line when a penalty kick is being taken. A technical foul within the large rectangle by a defender will result in a free from the centre of the thirteen metre line.

November 20th

Limerick appear in their first All-Ireland Senior hurling final on this this day in 1898 beating Kilkenny to win the delayed 1897 championship. Limerick were represented by Kilfinnane and beat Tullaroan who represented Kilkenny, 6-8 to 1-0. It was Kilkenny's third time to make the final and still not win the All-Ireland.

Wexford win their first All-Ireland Senior hurling title on this day in 1910. Wexford, represented by Castlebridge, beat Limerick, represented by Castleconnell, by a score of 7-0 to 6-2. There was some controversy over the new rules with Limerick having a square ball goal ruled out and a similar goal being awarded to Wexford. Limerick appealed but Central Council upheld the result and Wexford won their first title in their fifth final appearance, including the home final of 1901. Several of the Wexford team, including the team captain Seán Kennedy who would also be captain for the footballers in 1915, would go on to win All-Ireland medals with the great four in a row Wexford football team.

November 21st

The Hogan Stand is named after a Tipperary player who was shot when British forces opened fire on those attending a match between Dublin and Tipperary, on this day in 1920 at Croke Park. The match was being played in aid of the Republican Prisoners' Dependants' Fund. Some argued that the GAA should have cancelled the match after Michael Collins' men had made an early morning strike against British Agents sent to hunt him down. The GAA felt cancelling the match would have suggested they were involved in the planning. Thirteen were killed at Croke Park on that day including three young supporters, aged fourteen and under.

John Joe O'Reilly of the Cornafean GAA club was the captain of the Cavan Senior football team who lifted the Sam Maguire twice, in 1947 when they beat Kerry at the Polo Grounds in New York, and again in 1948 when they beat Mayo. He died on this day in 1952 at the age of 32. He was named on the 1984 Football Team of the Century, to mark the centenary of the GAA, at centre half back and was celebrated in a song of the time 'The Gallant John Joe.'

November 22nd

'But what really drove home why Sunday's All-Ireland semi-final should have been postponed was the almost total indifference exhibited by my southern colleagues.' John Haughey 'Irish News' Gaelic games correspondent in the wake of the Omagh bombing.

Of the Galway team that contested the first All-Ireland Hurling final in 1887 at least four had been evicted from their homes within a year and another Paddy Larkin went to jail for taking the hay of an evicted widow to market to sell on her behalf.

The Rules Today

When within the small rectangle, the goalkeeper cannot be charged but can be challenged for possession of the ball and his kick or pass can be blocked. Incidental contact with the goalkeeper while playing the ball is allowed.

November 23rd

'In past years we could have highlighted emigration as a factor and maybe to a small degree this is still a factor, but I feel that other matters such as lack of motivation, vision, commitment, personnel, identity and loyalty is very much evident within some club areas.' Donegal secretary Noreen Doherty on this day in 2005 on the challenges facing clubs.

Tipperary Senior hurling titles: 1887, 1895, 1896, 1898, 1899, 1900, 1906, 1908, 1916, 1925, 1930, 1937, 1945, 1949, 1950, 1951, 1958, 1961, 1962, 1964, 1965, 1971, 1989, 1991, 2001.

'When I would go down there to Crossmaglen, I would get out of the helicopter on a GAA field and run to the police station which was heavily fortified. For my money, that's bandit country. It was a bit like the Wild West.' Toby Harnden, author for 'Bandit Country,' justifies the title of his book.

November 24th

‘You’d have a couple of county medals and start to feel confident and then realise you were talking to lads who had as many or twice as many All-Ireland medals as you had county medals. You gave them respect and they taught with love and affection and pure hurling.’ John Meyler former Cork hurler.

‘He was the most famous voice in Ireland during his career. He meant everything to people of my age especially. There was very little transport during the war years so we had to stay at home and listen to the games on the radio and it was Micheál whose voice we heard. He made us familiar with all the great players, even though we never saw them, and you can still feel the same magic when you hear an old recording of his.’ Jack Boothman, President of the GAA, on Micheál Ó Hehir who passed away on this day in 1996.

November 25th

A daily newspaper report of the 1905 Railway Shield game between Leinster and Munster claimed Kildare footballer Mick Fitzgerald kicked a point from 85 yards!

Of the €70 charged for general admission to the All-Ireland Senior football final in 2008 €12.60 was redistributed among counties and provinces, €18.90 went to infrastructure investment, €9.10 to administration costs, €9.80 to player injury and welfare, €9.80 to match day costs and €9.10 to games development.

The Rules Today

In the event of extra-time in a drawn game any player sent off during the replay cannot be brought back on but another player can be brought on as a replacemnet.

November 26th

'Bertie Ahern had said to me before the budget when I told him I was going to do this, he recalled about the £5 million he had given previously "I was pilloried from one end of the country to the other and there was ferocious media opposition to it". So I was warned, but I thought some of the opposition was a bit hysterical.' Charlie McCreevey, the then Minister for Finance, on the reaction to him giving £2 million to the GAA in the 1998 budget.

The Rules Today

In football a player can carry the ball for no more than four consecutive steps or the time needed to take four steps. The ball can then be toe-tapped or bounced. A ball can only be bounced once on being caught and therafter once following each toe-tap. A ball not caught can be bounced more than once in succession. The ball may be changed from one had to the other providing the original hand remains in contact until the change has been made. The ball may be tossed for a kick, toe-tap or hand pass, the later must consist of a clear striking action with the open hand or fist.

November 27th

Dublin beat Galway in the 1983 Senior football Final with twelve men after having three players sent off.

Michael Cusack the founder of the GAA died on this day in 1906 at the age of fifty-nine.

'The main thing is, they'd eat grass to win. That's what I want. I'm not interested in lads ringing me up saying that they can't train because they need a babysitter, or their mother is not well, or there's someone after passing away.' Larry Tompkins, Cork Manager.

'I felt that Galway's culture, well, a good part of it, is a positive culture, a self-belief culture. I tried to tap into that as best I could.' Galway manager John O'Mahony on All-Ireland success in 1998.

November 28th

‘I’m not tempted. I spent enough time on the treatment table this year.’ Peter Canavan on why he is not tempted to keep playing inter-county football after his retirement in 2005.

Limerick Senior hurling titles: 1897, 1918, 1921, 1934, 1936, 1940, 1973.

The declaration rule is introduced in 1928 meaning that players can play for their county of birth rather than where they are resident. This gradually removes the situation where players win medals for different counties over a short period of time.

‘If we can make our own laws with reference to our pastimes, we can make our own laws in more serious matters.’ Michael Davitt 1890 on the rules brought in by the GAA.

November 29th

Kerry win their second All-Ireland Senior football title in a row when they beat Wexford in a replay in Croke Park, on this day in 1914, 2-3 to 0-6. As in the first game Wexford had a strong lead before a comeback from Kerry. As in the first game the comeback came in the form of a Paddy Breen goal saving the day for the Kingdom. P.D. Breen, the future president of the GAA, came on as a sub for Wexford in the second half.

'I just don't ever want to talk about myself in any great detail, other people in the GAA see that as part of their duty, maybe even a bonus. For me, I can't feel comfortable doing it. I don't see the necessity for talking in detail about myself. I manage a football team. How I do that should be evident from the results.' Former Derry manager and Dublin footballer Brian Mullins defines how managers should be interpreted.

November 30th

‘The great thing that came out of the Rule 42 issue was that the democratic nature of the Association was enhanced. Maybe for the first time the grass roots took hold of the situation themselves.’ Former GAA President Seán Kelly.

Westmeath are known as the Lake county or Lakesiders. They have won no titles at Senior level but have a Junior title in both hurling and football alongside an Under 21 title in football.

‘I’m disgusted with the county board. Look at our performance. See what it takes to beat Kilkenny because they can’t do it . . . It’s not that I want the job, but if they want to keep Offaly hurling alive they should have appointed me to the job.’ Pad Joe Whelehan the Birr manager on the Offaly County Board after his team beat Young Ireland’s in the Leinster club hurling final in 2002, Birr went on to win the club title for the second time in a row the following March.

December 1st

Kerry beat Kildare for the second time in a Senior final in the same year on this day in 1929 when they won the National League football title, 1-7 to 2-3. The Kingdom had already disposed of Kildare in the All-Ireland just over two months earlier. 11,000 spectators turned out to watch the match in Croke Park.

Lorenzo Ignatius Meagher, or Lory as he was known, of the Tullaroan club in Kilkenny captained the Senior team when they won the 1935 All-Ireland hurling final at the age of thirty-six making it his third time to win an All-Ireland Senior medal. He was named on the Team of the Millennium in the midfield position in 1999.

'Despite all the pleas, we still have far too many instances of a lack of discipline on the playing field and off it.' We had a number of instances at club and county level during the year which did serious harm to the image of our games.' Liam Mulvihill former GAA Director-General speaking in 1986.

December 2nd

Jimmy Doyle of Thurles Sarsfields was captain of the Senior Tipperary hurlers when they won the All-Ireland in 1962 and in 1965 beating Wexford on both occasions. He won six All-Ireland medals in total winning his first at the tender age of eighteen but most famously in 1961 he played in the final despite a broken ankle scoring nine points to help the Premier county beat Dublin 0-16 to 1-12.

John O'Leary the Dublin football goalkeeper retired in 1997 having played in seventy consecutive Senior championship games from July 1980 to June 1997.

'To Philip Jordan and Mattie Forde, I apologise sincerely to you guys. I'd like to say to them that I can't believe it was me doing those things - it's not the way that I play the game.' Australia's Chris Johnson on his clothes line tackle in the International Rules second test in 2005.

December 3rd

'His suggestion that he had to approach me on several occasions during the recent Munster final and ask me to cool it and stop abusing his players is both a downright untruth and beggars belief.' Gerald McCarthy the Waterford manager responds to claims by Ger Loughnane in 1998.

'I have never seen an organisation so hidebound by bullshit.' Wexford hurling manager Liam Griffin on the GAA

'The GAA - a haven of drunkeness and injury.' Diarmuid Ferriter Irish historian and author.

'I could give you examples of Aodan O Se's bar where it is choc-a-bloc for Manchester United and Liverpool.' Pat Comer of Galway on the challenge to traditional games in the Gaeltacht.

December 4th

Mike Sheehy of Austin Stacks club in Kerry is remembered by many as the player who chipped Dublin goalkeeper Paddy Cullen with a quickly taken free in the 1978 All-Ireland final scoring a goal that helped secure a seventeen point winning margin, 5-11 to 0-9. He also missed a penalty in the 1982 final against Offaly that would have secured a record five in a row for the Kingdom, they lost 1-15 to 0-17. He won a remarkable eight All-Ireland Senior football medals making his debut at Senior level in 1973 and retiring in 1988. His last came in 1986 and surprisingly Kerry would not win another until 1997.

Westmeath won their first ever Leinster Senior football final in 2004 when they beat Laois after a replay.

'I'm always suspicious of games where you're the only ones that play it.' Jack Charlton on hurling.

December 5th

Kerry won the All-Ireland Senior football final on this day in 1909 beating Louth, who had not appeared in a final since the very first in 1887, 1-9 to 0-6. Maurice McCarthy scored the only goal of the game in the first championship to finish in the same year it had started. Both teams were due to appear in the final again in 1910 but the title was awarded to Louth when Kerry refused to travel due to a dispute with the Great Southern and Western Railway over facilities for players.

'You are all young enough to come back next year.' Mick O'Dwyer the Kildare manager after they lost the 1998 final, they have not appeared in a final since.

Irish rugby international Eric Elwood played championship football for Galway in 1989.

December 6th

'After a year which can best be described as an 'annus horribilis' it is with some trepidation that I present my annual report to the 2006 Convention.' Roscommon County Board secretary Frank Dennehy reports on a tough year for the county on this day in 2006.

'Don't think they saw it in Fiji. Still in the dark ages there, they're still on the wireless. We'll send them a tape but they'll be delighted, like.' Seán Og Ó hAlpin the Cork hurler on whether his Fijian relatives were watching the All-Ireland final in 1999, which Cork won.

'Nights running around Augher with no lights on. Think I was crying through most of them. I'm glad of them now though.' Ryan McMenamin on the reward of hard training, speaking after his team won the 2008 All-Ireland Senior football final against Kerry, 1-15 to 0-14.

December 7th

'That was up another two levels from what they played against Cork. I'll never forget what I saw so close to me yesterday. The f***ing aggressiveness in the tackle was unreal, absolutely incredible.' Davy FitzGerald the Waterford manager on the sheer power of the Kilkenny hurling team in the 2008 final when they beat his side.

'They had fellas going down taking injuries every time we got up to goal. That's just experience and that's just what they kept doing. It's impossible to play against.' Cork captain Derek Kavanagh on the experience of Kerry footballers.

'Do we want to be the boys, in twenty years time that let Kerry win the three-in-a-row or do we want to be remembered as the team that stopped Kerry. He put that to a lot of the boys today. And I think we responded in style.' Ryan McMenamin of Tyrone explains how Mickey Harte motivated them to a third All-Ireland Senior football title, when they beat Kerry in 2008 1-15 to 0-14.

December 8th

Dublin and Cork met in the National League hurling decider on this day in 1929 in which the reigning All-Ireland champions were outscored by the Dubs in a game that saw twelve goals. Despite Paddy Aherne of Cork knocking in three goals Tom Burke of Dublin scored three of his own to help Dublin power to a 7-4 to 5-5 victory.

Richard Barrett a former Cork hurler and footballer is shot on this day in 1923 in a reprisal shooting by Free State troops.

'To treat our top stars in such a substandard and haphazard way in this day and age is absolutely ridiculous.' Dessie Farrell Dublin footballer.

Four out of the seven-member committee who founded the GAA were IRB men.

December 9th

Wexford win their third All-Ireland Senior title in a row, matching Dublin's record, on this day in 1917. They beat Clare, who were appearing in their first final, 0-9 to 0-5. For the second year in a row Kerry had withdrawn from the championship.

'As I get older I treasure it a bit more. When I was younger I took it for granted but I suppose every time we go out on the field it's a case of I don't want this to end today. I think that is a big driving force for us.' Oisín McConville, of Crossmaglen Rovers on the pursuit of the Senior county title prior to winning their twelfth in a row in 2007.

'He was a great man to motivate a team. It was a gradual thing, very thorough, he didn't just go in for the speech beforehand. As a manager, he had the perfect temperament.' Seanie Walsh of Kerry on Mick O'Dwyer.

December 10th

Wexford are known as the Slaneysiders, the Model county or the Yellow Bellies and have six Senior titles in hurling and five in Senior football. They won their first All-Ireland hurling final in 1910 without scoring a point but seven goals was enough to see off Limerick

'Just when a team was needed in Croke Park, along comes Waterford. I see a lot of ourselves in Waterford, just as hungry, just as skilful and just as well coached.' Ger Loughnane the Clare manager after the drawn Munster hurling final in 1998.

'I see life as an experiment. When you win, you don't do everything right and when you lose, you don't do everything wrong, but we did enough right today to get by.' Mickey Harte the Tyrone manager on winning the All-Ireland Senior football final in 2008.

December 11th

'The minute you start to feel happy with yourself, it all disintegrates.' Joe Brolly Derry footballer on the dangers of overconfidence.

Philip Larkin became the third generation of his family to win an All-Ireland hurling medal when Kilkenny beat Offaly 5-15 to 1-14 in the final following his father's and grandfather's footsteps.

In November 1909 Michael Collins was sworn into the IRB in London, by his fellow post office worker Sam Maguire, in whose honour the All-Ireland football trophy is named.

Liam Currams was a member of the first Offaly team to win an All-Ireland Senior hurling final in 1981 when they beat Galway 2-12 to 0-15 but he was also on the losing team when Offaly were beaten by Kerry in the football final in the same year.

December 12th

Tipperary were beaten for the first time in an All-Ireland Senior hurling final, on this day in 1909, when they lost to Kilkenny, 4-6 to 0-12. Bill Hennebry scored three of the Cats goals and goalkeeper Jim Dunphy kept Tipperary from scoring a goal, another unfortunate first for the Premier county, who up to this had scored a goal in every final they appeared in. For Kilkenny it was a signal they were now a major force in hurling. The next time Tipperary would win an All-Ireland the Cats would be two titles behind them and had surpassed Cork.

'I am probably after the most difficult year of my life with everything that has gone on in it and I wasn't able to say anything. I still won't say anything.' Davy Fitzgerald, the Clare goalkeeping legend, remains tight lipped on the controversy in Waterford hurling after guiding Waterford to the All-Ireland and his exit from the Clare Senior panel.

December 13th

'We were just after winning the All-Ireland and I believed he had shown himself the most successful trainer in the game. But he was snubbed.' Eoin 'Bomber' Liston on why he didn't travel for the 1986 Australian Rules tour under the management of Kevin Heffernan as he felt Mick O'Dwyer had been unfairly overlooked for the manager's job.

Tony Wall who captained Tipperary to an All-Ireland Senior hurling win in 1958, when they beat Galway 4-9 to 2-5, was also the recipient in that year of the first Texaco Hurler of the Year Award.

The biggest problem you have with young players is not whether they have the ability to play, but whether they have the strength of character to perform on big days.' Pat O'Shea the Kerry Senior football manager.

December 14th

Mick Gill wins the second of two All-Ireland Senior hurling medals in the same year on this day in 1924 when he played on the winning Dublin team against Galway. Only two months earlier he had played on the winning Galway team for the delayed finish to the 1923 Senior hurling championship when Limerick were beaten. The score on this day was 5-3 to 2-6 with Dublin's non playing captain being the first and only man to lift the trophy without taking to the field in the final.

Dublin Senior Hurling titles: 1889, 1917, 1920, 1924, 1927, 1938.

Kerry appear in their first All-Ireland Senior football final, on this day in 1913, since they stood down from the 1910 final in a dispute with a railway company. Kerry took no chances and their captain, Dick 'Dickeen' Fitzgerald, outscored the opposition when he scored 1-1 in the first half. The final score was Kerry 2-2 to Louth's 0-3.

December 15th

'Of the most pressing concern must be the continued decline in attendances at most of the major games. This problem did not suddenly appear this year; indeed it has been evident for a number of years and has accelerated since the advent of 'live' television coverage of the big national games.' 1983 report to Congress.

The town of Ballaghderreen which sent Seán Flanagan to captain Mayo to their last two All-Ireland successes, in 1950 and 1951, is actually in Roscommon for local government purposes. Only in the GAA's atlas is it part of Mayo.

'Tyrone are the team of the decade. There is no doubt about it I think. Does that answer your question?' Brian McGuigan of Tyrone replying to questions on his team's standing in the modern game, after they won their third All-Ireland Senior football title in 2008.

December 16th

'We don't play Gaelic football.' John Taylor, UUP Minister August 1996.

In olden times two distinct forms of hurling were played in Ireland, Camán known as summer hurling and Camánacht, winter hurling. The first using a hurl similar to today and allowing use of the hand but not restricted to a field of play while winter hurling had a restricted field of play and the ball could only be struck with a stick more similar to a hockey stick.

'It's a bit of a clash like Manchester United against Wimbledon, the aristocrats against the dour, dogged.' Pat Spillane before the 2002 All-Ireland Senior football final between Kerry and Armagh, Armagh won 1-12 to 0-14.

December 17th

'I feel much honoured by the Resolution adopted at the Thurles meeting, and I accept with appreciation the position of patron of the Association which has been offered to me.' Charles Stewart Parnell responds to Michael Cusack on this day in 1884 becoming one of the first patrons of the GAA.

Wexford win their second All-Ireland Senior football final in a row on this day in 1916. The final had been delayed by the Rising of the same year and was played on a frozen pitch in front of one of the smallest crowds in recent history. In a year of troubles Kerry had withdrawn from the championship in a dispute over money and Dublin were unable to field a team as a result of the Rising.

Football was played on the frozen Liffey in Dublin in 1740

December 18th

‘I beg to acknowledge the receipt of your communication inviting me to become a patron of the Gaelic Athletic Association, of which you are, it appears, the Hon Secretary. I accede to your request with the utmost pleasure.’ Dr. Thomas William Croke, Archbishop of Cashel agrees to become patron of the newly formed GAA on this day in 1884.

The Polo Grounds New York, the home of the New York Giants until they moved to San Francisco in 1957 hosted the 1947 All-Ireland football Final.

‘Old men have forgotten the miseries of the Famine and had their youth renewed by the sights and sounds that were evoked by the thrilling music of the camán, the well directed stroke of the Cúl Báire, or the swift stride of the Gaelic forward in his pursuit of the ball to victory.’ Michael Davitt 1884

December 19th

‘When I was appointed to the job by a margin of about thirty-sixteen, I realised that I wasn’t going into a totally straightforward situation.’ John O’Mahony the former Galway football manager after winning the All-Ireland in 1998 points out his appointment wasn’t unanimous.

Wicklow are known as the Garden County and while they have no Senior All-Ireland titles they have won two Junior titles in both hurling and football.

‘I felt it was the zenith of Dublin’s power at that time. We were more or less going to be finished one way or another in ‘78 because of the age of the team.’ Tony Hanahoe the Dublin player-manager and captain when they won the 1977 All-Ireland Senior football final having beaten Kerry in the semi-final and Armagh in the final.

December 20th

'The defeat by Mayo in the 1951 final was a great disappointment. The Meath team was going to America the week following the match and the players were inoculated and some of them reacted badly to the injection and we were beaten by 2-8 to 0-9.' Peter McDermott of Meath on their defeat giving Mayo two All-Ireland's in a row, Meath lost again in 1952 in a replay to Cavan.

'Those who say that no sports organisation in the Ireland of today should have such a ban should remember that no other Irish sporting organisation had to suffer the events of the first Bloody Sunday or the type of regular and well documented harassment inflicted on GAA clubs in the Six Counties.' Congress report in 1995 where a motion to remove Rule 21 failed.

'Another factor is the fact that Croke Park is tighter than Munster pitches, games are more physical in Croke Park.' Jamesie O' Connor on playing at headquarters.

December 21st

Wexford won the Leinster Senior football final in 1893 when their Kilkenny opponents refused to retake the field after half time claiming the play was too rough. In the second half of the All-Ireland final Cork left the pitch for the same reason and Wexford were declared the winners.

'There are many awkward positions in sport and in life. The more you get and the more you deal with you should only come out wiser. I wouldn't say it was an awkward decision, but it was an acute decision. You have to make a lot of acute decisions in sport, and this was just another one.' Tyrone Manager Mickey Harte on the Tyrone team accepting Stephen O'Neill back into the team in time for All-Ireland Senior football final in 2008.

'We're becoming too pansyish about our football. It's a game for men, for God's sake.' Mick O' Dwyer on sending offs in Gaelic football.

December 22nd

Croke Park, then known as the Jones' Road Ground, was bought in 1908 for £3,250 by Frank Dineen, former GAA President and Secretary, who held it in trust for the organisation. The GAA become the official owners on this day in 1913 and named the ground Croke Park.

'Kerry and Kilkenny ruthlessly exploited their advantages this September. At this moment both are well ahead of the rest. They have set the standards in terms of preparation and motivation. Rather than complain about one-sided All-Irelands the others will have to raise their standards or these two will continue to dominate.' Jack O'Connor the former Kerry manager comments on the outcome of the 2007 Championships.

'You mustn't stand back or sit back, aloof, away from it. You must be part of it all. If you're not, you're not doing your job.' Micheál Ó Hehir on how to give the best commentary.

December 23rd

'I knocked over a few points. Sure that's what I'm there for. It's a pity I don't get paid for it.' Dan Shanahan the Waterford hurler.

'You're a hero when things go right, but when things go wrong you could end up in the lyrics of a song about the Ryder Cup captain.' Donal O'Grady Cork hurling manager in 2004, Cork won the All-Ireland so no songs about Bernard....

'It's definitely worked out well from a GAA point of view in terms of bigger games and greater exposure but personally I would prefer the old system and I think that's the general feeling in Offaly.' Johnny Dooley of Offaly who were the first team to win the All-Ireland Senior hurling title under the new back door system in 1998.

December 24th

‘No One.’ Christy Ring when asked who was marking him in the final ten minutes of the 1956 game against Limerick when he scored three goals.

Cork won the Munster Senior football final in 2008 despite being down eight points at half time with a spirited second half comeback winning the Munster crown 1-16 to 1-11. They almost did the same in the semi-final replay when they came back from nine points down to level the match against Kerry again but the Kingdom went on to win 3-14 to 2-13.

‘I think I took a lot of stick from one particular person yesterday who was waiting a long time to have a go at me. I think that really shows the person up for what he is and what he is about. Vendettas . . . there is no place for them in hurling.’ Davy FitzGerald the Waterford manager unhappy with some of the commentary the day after his side lost by twenty-three points to Kilkenny in the All-Ireland Senior hurling final in 2008.

December 25th

'He continues to raise the ante, from overall fitness to supporting the notion of some sort of financial reward for the players as the demands continue to grow.' Ger Power of Kerry on Mick O'Dwyer.

'The players were outstanding, they were terrific from start to finish and were totally focused, obviously. They hurled at a very serious level.' Brian Cody the Kilkenny Senior hurling manager on his teams performance in the 2008 final when they beat Waterford 3-30 to 1-13.

'If there is an injury, don't try to describe it ... particularly a head injury. The player's mother or wife or family might be listening and an ill informed or exaggerated comment could cause them unnecessary worry. Always remember the listener. Now, off you go.' Micheál Ó Hehir advice to a new radio commentator.

December 26th

'They must have got the plans out in California. I mean, the climate in Ireland is one of plenty wind and rain and if you go and sit at the front of the new stand where the Cusack once was, you will get drenched.' Mick O'Dwyer on the new Cusack Stand December 2000.

Wexford Senior Hurling titles: 1910, 1955, 1956, 1960, 1968, 1996.

'I will never forget that point. I think it was unreal. I'll look at that forever more. That was some feat, the man amazes me every day.' Mickey Harte, the Tyrone manager, discussing a Brian Dooher point in the 2008 All-Ireland Senior football final. The thirty-two year old team captain sprinted free of his marker to level the game 0-6 to 0-6, Tyrone went on to win 1-15 to 0-14.

December 27th

A letter from Archbishop Croke accepting the position of paton of the GAA is published in 'The Nation' newspaper on this day in 1884 giving the association, only a month old, a very important endorsement from the Catholic church in Ireland.

'That's the way I am. If you confront something straight away, you don't bear grudges. What you see with me is what you get.' Ger Loughnane.

'I'm stepping down after four years in charge of Dublin today, the bookies who were quoting them at three to one were off their heads.' Paul Caffrey former Dublin manager comments on the odds on Tyrone prior to a game where they beat Dublin by twelve points in the 2008 football championship.

December 28th

‘It’s ferocious, in a lot of counties, if you don’t play well in a match, you may not be playing the next day. In Kilkenny, if you don’t go well in training, you may be gone. There are lads breathing down your neck left right and centre. It does not matter whether you are corner back or corner forward.’ Kilkenny hurler Jackie Tyrrell on the competitive nature of hurling in the county.

‘We came here with all guns blazing and we just came up short. We will come back stronger for this. We maybe lacked a killer punch and that bit of experience of an All-Ireland semi-final stuff but you learn from that. The match hung on things. That is hurling.’ Liam Sheedy of Tipperary on losing a quarter-final to Waterford in 2008.

‘Take out the few late tackles and it’s not any harder than Gaelic.’ Kieran McGeeney the Armagh footballer on the International Rules.

December 29th

'Today we totally ignored the scoreboard. We wanted a good start and we got it. Eddie chipped in with a couple of auld goals there. We were relentless, to be honest. We never let up and that is why the margin was so big in the end.' Kilkenny captain James Fitzpatrick on a scoreline of 3-30 to 1-15 when they beat Waterford in the 2008 Senior hurling final.

Cavan won their second All-Ireland Senior football final in a row in 1948 against Mayo, 4-5 to 4-4. At one stage Cavan had been ahead by 3-2 to 0-0 but Mayo staged a recovery with Padraig Carney scoring the first penalty ever in an All-Ireland final.

'You guys would be lucky to touch it.' Australian coach Leigh Matthews on Ireland's chances in the International Rules series in 1998, Ireland under the management of Colm O'Rourke won the series 128 to 118.

December 30th

Jimmy Murray of the Roscommon club Knockcroghery was the captain of the county football team in 1943 when they won their first Senior Connacht title in twenty-nine years. Roscommon went on to their first ever appearance in an All-Ireland final winning a replayed final against Cavan 2-7 to 2-2. They were in the final again in 1944 and 1945 beating Kerry in the first but losing the 1945 final to the Kingdom.

'There were occasions when referees did not receive the due support they should have.' Joe McDonagh on a tough year for referees in 1999.

'Match of the decade, though that was no good to us because we didn't win it.' Eamonn Coleman describes a championship game between Derry and Down in 1994, Down went on to win the All-Ireland.

December 31st

Mick O'Connell of the Waterville club in Kerry won four All-Ireland Senior medals with the Kingdom. The island man from Valentia was captain of the Kerry team when they won the All-Ireland in 1959 beating Galway 3-7 to 1-4 and played his last All-Ireland final at the age of thirty-five when the Kingdom lost to Offaly in 1972.

'I don't believe you need the hardship. I believe you can get fit without killing yourself.' Clare hurler David Forde on Ger Loughnane's training regime.

'I'm only in the business of getting to the top. I'm a realist, and know it doesn't always happen. But if you don't believe it, how can you expect your players to believe it? You have to show the leadership, aspire to the top.' Mickey Harte the Tyrone manager on leadership.